ADVANCE PRAISE

"Allison is like an orchestra maestro, waving her baton at your positive thoughts and bringing their volume higher. Then she waves that magic wand over at your truth, at your creativity, at your confidence, at your perseverance, and she organizes it all into something you can *do*."

— KATYA LIDSKY, WRITER, ACTOR, ADVOCATE,
MOTHER, LOS ANGELES, CALIFORNIA

"Allison is an incredibly gifted coach. If you're ready to take that next step in life or just need help balancing on the step that you're on, trust Allison to be that powerful force to help you reach your goals sooner than you could have dreamed. She took our little dream of being real estate designers and investors and helped us launch our careers. We're now proud owners of investment properties and have a portfolio to boot."

— SARAH AND NICK KARAKAIAN, CO-OWNERS OF
NESTRS, COLUMBUS, OHIO

"Allison and I had four phone sessions over two months, and in that two months I had accomplished more on a personal level than I had ever before. Allison inspired me to go further than my goals, and as a result I am a happier person."

— RACHEL VINE, TELEVISION WRITER,
LOS ANGELES, CALIFORNIA

"My work with Allison began as I desired "more" out of life after having a baby. She helped me cast out self-doubt and together, we discovered my passion in life. Soon after, my husband and I began to see her for couples coaching. Allison helped us to uncover an amazing opportunity by relocating to another state. Since moving, life has been more rich, calm, and optimistic. I am so excited for what lies ahead and I owe this beautiful experience to Allison's guidance!"

— MICHELE MISSONELLIE, NUTRITIONIST,
ENTREPRENEUR, FORT WAYNE, INDIANA

"It was as if she knew my goals (and my potential) before I recognized them. Her life experience is unmatched, as she has lived every day to its fullest potential. And in doing so, she's inspired the people around her to follow suit."

— CARLY KINCANNON, OWNER, AMERICA'S
SWEETHEARTS, ASTORIA, NEW YORK

"I came to Allison during a difficult career transition, with a lot of questions and very few answers. She has a tried-and-true process that focused on me, my needs and my questions. I had a lot of balancing to do as a full-time career mom, and I was pleasantly surprised and grateful that her coaching touched all of the important areas of my life, from self, to career, to relationship, to family."

— LYNNETTE COLALILLO, USER EXPERIENCE
CONSULTANT, CEDAR GROVE, NEW JERSEY

"Allison helped me find my post-baby career identity during a time when I needed more than a friend or family member's ear. Because of her support and nonjudgmental approach, I have been able to accomplish 100% of what I set out to do in my work with her."

— LIZZY SWICK, OWNER, LIZZY SWICK NUTRITION,
MONTCLAIR, NEW JERSEY

"My Mount Everest, or "monster under the bed," as Allison humorously referred to it, was my financial situation. I could no longer run away from the frightening reality of it. Well, with Allison's guidance, encouragement, knowledge of resources, and positive approach, the topic of my finances became manageable and a little less scary. Since working with Allison, my life has improved in too many ways to name. I can say that my greatest achievement has been that I have stopped running away from whatever is thrown at me. I feel as though I am "plugged into life" again."

— MARIA S. CHASSEN, TEACHER, LYCÉE FRANÇAIS, MANHATTAN, NEW YORK

I started working with Allison at a point where my life was undergoing a major change, and I was struggling to find my path forward. Allison helped me organize my brain and my life, and in a careful, organized and forward-looking way, worked with me on a plan. I look ahead with renewed confidence and excitement. Thank you Allison!"

— ANDREW ROSENTHAL, EDITOR AND WRITER, MONTCLAIR, NEW JERSEY

PERSONAL
(R)EVOLUTION

ALLISON TASK

PERSONAL (R)EVOLUTION

HOW TO BE HAPPY, CHANGE YOUR LIFE, AND DO THAT THING YOU'VE ALWAYS WANTED TO DO

PEACH ELEPHANT PRESS

ISBN 978-0-9951103-1-1 (PAPERBACK)
ISBN 978-0-9951103-2-8 (KINDLE)

Personal (R)evolution: How to Be Happy, Change Your Life, and Do That Thing You've Always Wanted to Do

Cover and Author Image © Nick Levitin

First Printing, 2018
Peach Elephant Press

This book is for each of my clients.

I thank you for opening your hearts and minds and lives, and inviting me to help you be your best you.

Thank you for helping me realize my career goal, and for bringing the pages of this book to life with your stories.

CONTENTS

INTRODUCTION

x ◆→————————→ •

I'm Allison Task, career and life coach, and author of this book. Thanks so much for picking it up.

Before you jump in, I've got a question for you: Why did you pick up this book? It's a real question, something only you know, and it's important for the work we can do here. So kindly share your reason—say it out loud, write it down, or draw a picture:

Ok, thanks! That's helpful. If this book delivers on its promise and has the ability to take you from *here* (where you are now) to *there* (the reason you're reading this book as stated above), what would the latter look like? What's that situation you'd rather be in? And for this, kindly take as much time as possible and be as detailed as you can:

When I have my first session with a client, there is a reason they've walked through the door. There's something they want to do, to talk about, to change in their life. My goal with this book is to help you just like I help the clients I see in my office.

I want to help you do that thing you want to do.

And the best way to move towards it is to name it—to say what that thing is. So thank you for doing that.

A life coach helps you clarify where you are, where you'd rather be, and then helps you bridge the gap. I am a life coach, and I work with clients to do just that.

I wrote this book to compile all that I've learned coaching clients over the last decade plus and put it in one place, so more people would have access to the type of coaching I do—the coaching that has been so effective for my clients.

I sincerely thank you for picking up this book and giving my methods a shot.

I want this book to be helpful to you, to be an active tool, as if you've got your very own life coach in your pocket. Through this book, I want to do for you what I do in person for my coaching clients: become your accountability partner, a good question asker, holder of the vision of your best you, and clarifier of the Goal you want to achieve. While I may not *physically* be with you during your sessions, through this book you will enter an ongoing series of coaching conversations with me.

Together, we'll get real clear on what you want, determine why it's important to you, identify and remove whatever it is that's holding you back from achieving your Goal, and replace it with positivity, possibility, and momentum. Then we'll create a plan for how you'll get it, identify people you already know who can help you, and who you need to meet.

I believe in each person's potential to initiate positive change in their life. My goal with this book is to help you believe in that thing you want to do *and* your ability to do it, so you can make it happen. **Ready?**

WHAT IS COACHING?

You've probably worked with a coach at some point in your life—maybe it was a soccer or a baseball coach. They were different from a parent or a teacher. They helped you learn something, do something, gain a skill.

And then, if they were a good coach, they saw potential in you that you may not have seen in yourself. They saw something in you, carried a vision for what you could be, and helped you get there.

A coach collaborates with you to develop a vision of your best self: a vision of you based on your values, talents, and skills (existing or to be developed). Then that coach serves as an accountability partner and helps you realize that Goal.

It's a powerful relationship, fulfilling for both parties, I can assure you. It's not unusual that I check my email and get a message from a client that yes, he was offered (and accepted) that job as Head of School in Brazil; that yes, after that important conversation with her boyfriend, he proposed;

that he was offered that fellowship at Harvard he had been driving toward. My in-box is a joy to visit!

Coaching is not cheerleading, teaching, consulting, or therapy. A coach helps you conceive, navigate, and pursue your path.

You know when you watch the Olympics and someone just *nails* their performance? That's solid coaching. So when my clients achieve their Goal, we share that incredible feeling of joy. And that celebration, the recognition of the accomplishment, is part of the process (more about that in Chapter 9).

But wait, I'm getting ahead of myself. I geek out on Goal setting and Goal achievement, and the general badassness of my clients in general, one of which you are close to becoming. So forgive me. *And welcome to coaching.*

I've been waiting for you.

HOW DOES A COACH HELP?

Have you ever noticed how slow your computer becomes when you have too many programs open? Well, the same thing happens with your brain. When you're holding on to too many separate thoughts, ideas, or emotions, your mind moves slowly, and fresh thoughts (opening new programs) become more difficult. Much like your pokey computer, competing thoughts and negative emotions take up valuable processing energy until your thinking is sluggish.

As a coach, I help clients return efficiency and creativity to their thinking. By helping clients identify which thoughts are helpful, and which thoughts are less so, clients can "close" some of the programs they don't need (negativity, doubt, "should-talking"—more on that in Chapter 6). By closing some of the unnecessary "programs," we can free up space in your mind's RAM (random-access memory) to make room for the fresh, original thinking that will allow you to conceive new options and make changes.

I help my clients structure and prioritize their thoughts and ideas so new solutions can come forth.

John came to me because he was having a hard time choosing between two jobs. He had already prepared a list of pros and cons, and was still stuck. Together, we developed a weighting system for his list, based on his personal values and the importance of each category on his work/life balance, salary, sense of purpose, and commute. By asking John questions about his values, and weighting the criteria he had set, he was better able to navigate the puzzle of decision making with his own fresh thoughts.

Watching my clients engage in fresh thinking is a blast, like watching a baby take his or her first steps, or watching a gymnast finally nail a back flip. Have you ever seen an older child or adult experience snow for the first time? You can almost experience it with them! In fact, your brain is able to empathize with that freshness of experience, so you actually do experience it with them.

Fresh thinking is like a fresh spring breeze after a long winter, it lightens and lifts. With it, my clients foster the momentum that will carry them forward to take action and move toward their Goal.

Simply put: A coach helps you think (different).*

---

* Tip of the hat to Steve Jobs

WHY CHOOSE ME AS YOUR COACH?

You may be wondering what makes *me* qualified to be *your* coach. Well, as a certified life coach with more than 12 years of experience coaching private clients, I've helped hundreds of clients initiate positive change in their lives. And, in addition to helping others navigate major transitions, I've also experienced them myself.

I know firsthand how scary it can be to change your life. I also know how rewarding it is when you finally do! And the ride is much more joyful (and efficient) when there's someone to share it with. As your coach, I'll be with you every step of the way.

Here are some highlights:

I grew up as a pretty normal suburban kid in Rockville Centre, Long Island, New York. I was the oldest child, with a brother four years younger than me. My mom converted to Judaism after she met my dad. I mention this because I was raised Jewish in a town that could be tolerant of difference, and yet somewhat anti-Semitic at the same time, which was an interesting way to grow up. I was five when the first neighbor shut the door in my face, telling me she couldn't play with me because I was Jewish. I didn't completely understand the rejection. I did, however, learn from it.

These days, many experts tout the value of rejection, so I credit those early experiences (there were many more) with helping me build resilience. Rejection is a gift. The more you experience it—the more you get used to it and *still* persevere—the easier it will be to call on that skill throughout life. You'll need a strong cache of resilience in the face of rejection if you've got things you want to do in this life.

I was selected to be in the gifted and talented program in elementary school, which was nice—in part, due to the Pygmalion effect (which I'll describe more in depth in

Chapter 6). Simply put, the selection for this program in and of itself (regardless of my merit) gave me confidence, and it tended to make the teachers more confident in my skills and abilities. In high school, I was involved in track and drama and went on to study human development and family studies at Cornell University.

After college, I was intent on being a legal aid attorney—until my parents let me know that while college was on them, law school would be on me. At the time, I thought it seemed somewhat silly to get that deep into debt so early in my career.* I took my Ivy League degree straight to the local Italian restaurant and started waitressing while I interned at PBS in New York City. It wasn't long before I was hired as an executive assistant.

That was 1995, and the internet was starting to take off. I left my admin job after a year to become the eighth employee of EarthWeb, a New York-based internet company, and I took off on one of the wildest rides of my life. Within a year, I moved from New York to San Francisco and worked for a series of internet companies. I had a front-row seat to the explosion of California dotcom companies, complete with a chorus part in the performance. I was working with people who were literally inventing the internet. It was a heady, exciting time, and I saw what happened to people who believed in their visions and made the impossible a reality.

After almost a decade, as the dotcom leadership teams shifted from computer geeks (I use the term "geek" as a compliment) to the MBAs, I realized that tech didn't

---

* These days, most young adults are coming out of college deep in debt. The fact that I was able to make the choice at that time to *not* go into debt is in stark contrast to the number of young adults who are pressured into taking on debt without realizing the impact until they feel it in their 20s and 30s. Many of the young clients in my office today have a college loan debt of $30,000 to $300,000.

fundamentally excite me—no matter how thrilling the
early days were. Bits and bytes, computers and technology
just weren't my jam. I took a sabbatical and realized what I
actually wanted to do was learn to cook.

More precisely, I wanted to help young professional
women cook. Women who were smart, working, and were
likely shooed out of the kitchen by their mothers in the '80s
and '90s. Women who wanted to have careers and start a
family someday, and who had zero skills in the kitchen or with
homemaking in general. I knew this need existed, because I
was one of these women. At the time, I was so incompetent
in the kitchen that I couldn't even peel a hard-boiled egg. No
matter. I was determined to learn, and then to teach. Maybe
even to teach on television.

I quit the dotcom. And armed with money I had saved
working there, I took the big step of enrolling in culinary
school. There I sat in my interview with big bright eyes,
telling the school official about my plans: to cook, to teach,
to write cookbooks, and host my own TV cooking show. Her
response: "A lot of people want that."

Sure they did. I, however, was determined to be one
of the people who actually *did* that. And to make sure that
happened, my next move after culinary school was to go
work for Martha Stewart.

Yes, Martha Stewart herself, in the flesh, and she was just
as hardworking and intense as I had hoped for. In return, I
worked my tail off, always watching, listening, and learning.
I made the two-hour drive from Brooklyn to Connecticut
every day—and I loved it.

And that's how I accomplished one of my major goals: to
cook on TV. First, I was given the opportunity to audition
for a spot on "Everyday Food," a new show Martha was
pitching to PBS. I was offered the role. That led to several
years where I learned about cooking, television, and cooking

on television—just as the Food Network was on the rise. I eventually co-hosted "Home Made Simple" on Lifetime and "Cook Yourself Thin" on TLC. And I spent two years as the host of "Blue Ribbon Hunter" on Yahoo, which sent me around the United States learning about unusual food trends and attending, competing, and judging at food festivals.

It was a blast. I recognized how lucky I was to be taking this ride, and I promise you, I enjoyed and appreciated every last minute of it.

During that time, I opened my own cooking school, The Wooden Spoon, where I helped people in the New York area learn to cook in their very own kitchens.

If you're wondering how I had time to do the TV shows and the cooking school, let me explain. When I was given the opportunity to be on television, there were all kinds of crazy agreements I had to sign banning me from appearing on anything else for a year after the first airing of the show. Which meant I had to have side gigs to allow me to pursue the on-camera work. Remember how Prince had to change his name because he no longer owned his name or likeness? It was kind of like that—without all the purple and high heels. If I took advantage of the opportunity to be on camera, I would have to sit on the sidelines for the following year. Crazy, right?

It was while I was sitting on the sidelines that I discovered my next challenge. While appearing on TV may have been fun, teaching was meaningful. When I was in the home kitchens of my private cooking students, conversations veered from chopping shallots to getting married or having a better job.

I started to love these conversations more than the actual cooking. I enrolled in a program at New York University for personal and life coaching, and I became a certified coach.

In my early to mid-thirties, I was thoroughly enjoying my varied and evolving career. My personal life was another story. I wanted children, and a partner, and was running out of time for the former in a hurry. I started looking into becoming a single mother on my own.

And then I met a guy.

One stepchild, two sons, and one daughter later, I can say that I have satisfied my desire for children (and a husband). And that process taught me about infertility (and fertility) and being a working mom (and stepmom).

Today, my full-time job is working as a career and life coach. I am a coach practitioner, working with individuals in my Montclair, New Jersey office (and via Skype, Zoom, and phone for geographically distributed clients). It is a pleasure and an honor to foster the change my clients want to make.

I am the mother of three preschoolers and stepmother to a teenager. I am a wife, daughter, and friend, and an active volunteer and member of my community. I have deliberately chosen a career that I love, and which also gives me the ability to prioritize my family and life. I have a short commute and revenue that satisfies my needs.

All these years, all those people who saw limitations and told me "no" were reflecting their own limiting beliefs—from my anti-Semitic childhood neighbors to the culinary-school official who didn't take my goals seriously. I'd be damned if they were going to put those limits on me!

Now I spend my days breaking down false, limiting beliefs with my clients, so they can create the lives they want.

That's my story, and a bit more about how I got here. Now let's turn our attention back to you.

Ready?

HOW TO USE THIS BOOK

In Personal (R)evolution, I've assembled my favorite coaching tools, the ones that help my clients make significant breakthroughs and provide them with the momentum to move forward. The book is designed to be a series of coaching sessions, just like I have with my clients.

Each chapter of this book is designed to move you closer to achieving your Goal. Each chapter has a theme, tools, scientific evidence that backs up these concepts, and stories from real clients that show you how they've successfully applied these tools.

You may want to read through this book carefully, working through each exercise in the chapter before moving on to the next. Some exercises may not resonate with you. If they don't, feel free to skip them.

Or, you may want to read the book in one big sprint, and then return to the sections as you need them.

The chapters are filled with Reflection Stop Points, Action Stop Points, and lots of questions. The questions are designed to help you stimulate fresh thinking and take action. Use them.

Here's an overview of what you'll explore in each chapter:

ONE: Where Do You Want To Be? SMART Goal Setting. In this chapter, I'll help you dream big with respect to your Goal and identify why it's so important to you. You'll ensure your Goal is something you want and can realistically achieve using the **SMART** goal-setting technique. **SMART** is an acronym that stands for a Goal that is Specific, Measurable, Attainable, Relevant, and Time-bound.

TWO: Your Goal in the Context of Your Life: The Whole Life Model. Have you ever seen the t-shirt with our solar system and a little arrow that points to Earth with the phrase "You are here"? In this chapter, we'll do something like that—placing your Goal in the larger context of your life. You'll determine what you may need to do before you pursue your Goal, and how achieving it will impact your life and the lives of those around you.

THREE: C'mon Get Happy: Practice Happiness and Gain Momentum. Before you get down to business moving toward your ambitious Goal, I want to help you get into an optimal Goal-pursuing frame of mind. This chapter shares research in the growing field of happiness and practical tools you can put to use immediately.

FOUR: Identify & Connect with Your Network. Now that you're feeling good, it's time to reach out and share your big dream with those you love. Chapters 4 and 5 help you connect with your network. They are especially powerful for those who hate the idea of networking.

FIVE: Connect with and Expand Your Network. In the previous chapter, you probably connected with some wonderful old friends and feel great about it. Now you'll begin to pursue people you don't know (yet). I'll help you with your elevator pitch and key talking points about what you want and what you have to offer.

SIX: Frameworks that Elevate Your Thinking and Inspire Momentum. Chapters 4 and 5 helped you connect with and expand your network. Chapters 6 and 7, the action chapters, will help you clarify your thinking and take strong action. This chapter will provide you with conceptual frameworks that lead to Insights. This shift in thinking will move you toward your Goal.

SEVEN: Doubt Crusher: Tactical Tools to Help You Break Through and Take Action. This is the chapter where you make things happen. This chapter is, in fact, the engine of change, and will bring you to the precipice of your goal.

EIGHT: Close the Deal. The finish line is in sight. You've done the work and the Goal is almost yours. This chapter will help you step back, acknowledge the work you've done and why you've done it—and then take that final leap toward your Goal.

NINE: Celebrate, Rest, and Repeat. Acknowledging and celebrating is an important part of the coaching process; it reinforces what you've done so you can do it again. This is the chapter where you do reflect and celebrate. Then you share your win in such a way that your new network shares in your achievement! Afterwards, you take a good long nap and let it soak in. From fiesta to siesta, this chapter helps you tie it all up with a bow.

As you move through each chapter, you will have your "aha moments," where you have a fresh thought and they are important. I refer to them as Insights. During these moments you create a fresh connection in your brain, and you want to reinforce it, as it will become a springboard for action.

So please highlight, underline, circle, or sticky-note the points that resonate with you. And write down your fresh thoughts, or Insights, as you go. Just like a well-loved cookbook, this book will get messy.

Many of the exercises suggested in the book are writing or thinking. If speaking into a recorder is easier than writing, do that. Or capture your response on video. Or if you want to work with an accountability partner and talk it out with someone who is a good listener, do that. Use whatever tools help you think.

The thinking exercises are called Reflection Stop Points, and the writing and more active exercises are called Action Stop Points. You may want to have a separate notebook where you can delve deeper into your thoughts. Whether that's your iPad or a Moleskine notebook, it doesn't matter. You do you! Go deep, follow new thoughts, and pursue fresh ideas as far as they'll take you.

There will be plenty of questions, and the more effort you make with your responses, the more efficiently you'll progress toward your Goal.

At the end of each chapter, there is a section called Insights & Actions. Insights is the place to consolidate any new ideas you have. Look back on the chapter. What did you underline? What did you write in your margins? What are your key takeaways and headlines? If you wanted to shift your thinking this week in three to five areas, what would they be?

The Actions section is where you give yourself a road map for tangible Actions to take before starting the next chapter. Throughout the chapter you've had ideas for Actions you want to take now or in the coming weeks—people you can call, web sites you want to check out, or something you need to Google. These are Actions you want to take that will help you move toward your Goal. Ideally, you will have identified at least three to five Actions you can take in each chapter that will help you realize your Goal. These Actions will be based on your original thinking and Insights. Record and commit to the Actions that you will take before you begin the next chapter.

My in-person coaching clients know the Insights &
Actions routine well. One wall of my office is painted with
whiteboard paint. Throughout our coaching session, I record
their Insights and Actions on the wall while they speak. At
the end of the session, I ask the question, "What was useful
to you during this session? What thoughts do you have now
that you didn't have an hour ago?" They are able to tease out
the Insights they've had in the last hour, record them, and
reinforce those thoughts.

My clients also identify the Actions they want to take
before our next session, whether that's jogging two miles each
day or calling their five closest friends and sharing their Goal.

The Insights & Actions section is where you capture and
confirm your Insights, translate them into tangible Actions
and hold yourself accountable for moving forward.

And one last thing. Each time, before you move on to
the following chapter, kindly complete your prep sheet (it's
easy, just seven questions). Remember that question I asked
at the very beginning of this chapter, "Why did you pick up
this book?" That was your prep for the book—you prepared
yourself for the book by exploring the reason you picked up
the book in the first place.

Just like that line you wrote at the beginning of this intro,
your pre-chapter prep helps you focus your thinking for each
phase and helps you monitor your progress while you go.

Okay. Enough preamble. It's time to turn that page, grab
your pen, and get ready to do some life-changing work. If
you want to achieve your Goal, let's turn your Insights into
Action.

Ready? Of course you are. Let's do this!

PREP SHEET

Prior to each coaching session, I ask my coaching clients to complete a prep sheet. This gives them the opportunity to reflect on the Actions they committed to, share their successes, and identify any potential obstacles.

Most importantly, it gives my clients the opportunity to set an agenda for the session before we begin. By determining what they want to do in our time together, we can more effectively accomplish it.

Please complete this before you begin the next chapter:

MY GOAL IS:

WHERE AM I, ON A SCALE OF 1 TO 10, TOWARD ACHIEVING MY GOAL?

If, when you picked up this book and just started thinking about your Goal for the first time in this process, you were at a 1, how far along are you now?

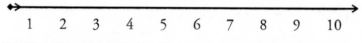

WHAT HAVE I ACCOMPLISHED SINCE I BEGAN READING THE INTRO CHAPTER?

WHAT OPPORTUNITIES ARE AVAILABLE TO ME RIGHT NOW?

BY THE END OF THE NEXT CHAPTER I WANT TO:

_____

_____

ANY INSIGHTS OR NEW AWARENESS THAT EXCITES ME?

_____   _____

_____   _____

ONE

WHERE DO YOU WANT TO BE?
SMART GOAL SETTING

WHERE DO YOU WANT TO BE?
SMART GOAL SETTING

x ✦⟩————————⟶ ●

Every reader picks up this book for one of two reasons:
1. You know where you want to be
2. You know where you *don't* want to be

You're moving *toward* something or moving *away* from something. A book like this speaks to people who want to take action and, for whatever reason, have not been able to (yet).

In the intro, you shared why you picked up this book. The goal of this chapter is to clarify what you need to do and how you need to do it to obtain your Goal. I will ask powerful questions to get your juices flowing, and by the end of the chapter you'll have refined your Goal using the SMART goal-setting technique.

My questions are designed to help you dig deep and create new thoughts. Please don't answer them superficially, as tempting as it may be. Truly stop and think for a moment, and you'll discover new ideas and connections in your thinking (those powerful "aha moments"). These connections may come to you while you answer the question, tomorrow morning in the shower, or while you're walking the dog. Throughout the course of our coaching, your head will be buzzing with fresh thoughts.

As you work through this chapter, please keep in mind that coaching work takes time, and that time is active. Unlike passive activities like watching a movie or reading a novel, you're the author of this story. You are in the driver's seat and you can decide where you want to go. **Take the wheel.**

Please set aside the time this process needs, about two to five hours per week. Use that time to read the chapter, reveal and capture your Insights, complete the Reflection and Action Stop Points and any additional Actions you assign yourself. I believe wholeheartedly in the effectiveness of positive thinking as long as it's accompanied by action.

My clients achieve their Goals by using the inspiration from Insights to create momentum that leads to Actions.

LEARN YOURSELF TO FIND YOUR GOAL

People often come to me in stress. Something in their life is not working as they'd like it to. My first job is to probe their desire for change, to learn more about where they are coming from, and why now.

And so I ask you: Why now? Why, specifically, today? Why not a month ago? Why do you have urgency?

In my office, clients often arrive ready to share. Some may talk for the first twenty to thirty minutes of our first session. I record their comments, put some structure to it, and ask a deeper level of question.

Amalia was a high-achieving client with a Harvard law degree and a young child. Her challenge: she hated practicing law. She's not alone; many lawyers do. In addition, she had crushing debt—over $300,000 of it.

In our first conversation, she asked the following questions: "How can I not pursue the law? How will I repay my debts? How can I let down my parents who supported my ambition?" As a woman of both Latin and African-American descent, she felt a sense of obligation to excel in her field.

And then she detailed how practicing the law made her physically sick. She shook her head in disbelief that she had come to this point. "I am a disappointment to myself, to my parents, to Latinas and African-Americans."

As her coach, I asked the following questions, one at a time, with long pauses between so that she could respond:

If you weren't a "disappointment," what would you be?

What is the opposite of disappointment?

Who, for you, is an example of that opposite quality?

How would you describe someone who chooses to speak with a coach to address these concerns?

What do you think of someone with a Harvard law degree who stops practicing law?

Do you know anyone who has?

If your child came to you in twenty-five years with these questions, how would you respond?

She looked to the side and took her time with each question. I could tell that these questions stimulated fresh thoughts in her mind. She started talking about bravery and authenticity, and recognized that she didn't know a lot of people who left law. She gave herself the action item of finding some of those people who left law for other careers; she began identifying role models who could motivate her.

●◦→————————→ ❋

It's time for you to move forward and start answering your own questions. Let's access those deeper, more powerful original thoughts. Let's put the magnificent engine of *your* brain to use for you. Ready?

WHAT'S GOING RIGHT WITH YOUR LIFE?

Let's take a step back and look at what is going right with your life. Imagine if you went to your doctor with a sore throat, and your doctor said to you, "Your muscle tone is incredible, your weight is perfect, your eyesight is actually better than most people your age. This sore throat is surmountable, and we'll fix it." How comforting would that be? You might even heal a bit faster knowing how well your body works.

Goal setting can become so focused on fixing and improving the thing that isn't working right now that you can overlook how much you've got going for you. Let's shift your thinking to a more positive state and focus on the good things you're doing—what's going well.

REFLECTION STOP POINT:

× When's the last time you had a great laugh? What caused it?

× What are you most proud of professionally right now?

× What kind of awards or accomplishments have you received? Think about when you found out you were getting it—take yourself through the whole story.

× What is one of your best traits? Another? And another?

× Who is someone you have a strong relationship with? Why did you choose them? Why did they choose you?

LOOK BACKWARD TO LOOK FORWARD

One grounding exercise that you can try is to look back at your early passions and interests, the things you were proud of and the areas where you excelled when you were little or in high school. Are those foundational affinities still in your life?

This reflection doesn't only need to focus on positive achievements. Even challenges or obstacles you faced—and overcame—can be illuminating and lead to positive memories of resilience or character building.

REFLECTION STOP POINT:

× Did you used to love music or dancing? When's the last time you saw live music, played an instrument or danced?

× Did you ever paint? What did you like about it? Which of the visual arts appealed to you?

× Did you receive awards for writing? Singing? A musical instrument? Anything else? What?

× Was there a situation when someone said "no" to something you wanted to do, and you did it anyway? Recount the whole story, beginning to end.

Looking back at your younger self and the things that were important to you early in your life can be a very helpful way to identify opportunities in your present, and ways you can reconnect with yourself. If you are feeling unhappy, simply recalling the last time you were happy—and the details of that day—can help you feel more like yourself. Reliving the memory helps you reconnect to those positive feelings and bring them into the present.

Don't worry, I won't tell you to quit your job and become a musician just because you loved drumming as a child. Recognizing these deep-seated passions, however, can be useful in remembering components of what makes you, you. If you structure your thinking around these formative interests and passions, you'll find yourself standing on more solid ground.

REFLECTION STOP POINT:

× When you were a child, how did you like to play? Alone? In groups? What were the games you played or invented? How did you play them? Who were your friends, and why did you choose them?

× As a teenager, what were the things you could do for hours without noticing time passing?

× Describe a time in your life when you felt confident. What made you feel that way?

× If you could time travel back to any age between birth and twenty years, which age would you choose? Now that you're that age again, how would you spend your day?

CONCEIVE A SPECTACULAR FUTURE

If you picked up this book because you're feeling restless or unsatisfied, one way to flip that feeling and find more ease is to ask yourself what a better future would look like. You know if you're unhappy in your relationship or at your job, perseverating on that unhappiness magnifies it. Like Amalia, when you focus on your positive future, what a better situation looks like, you can begin to build it. Conceiving the future is the first step toward building it. Replace overload and anxiety with excitement and motivation.

REFLECTION STOP POINT:

× If you had a magic wand and the power to change your current situation, what would you point that wand at? What specific changes would you make?

These are questions only you can answer; you are the expert on you. They are important, so take your time with them. I anticipate that answering these questions will take at least an hour if done thoughtfully and thoroughly.

RESUME VS. EPITAPH

David Brooks' recent best-selling book, *The Road to Character*, opens with a discussion of the resume-self versus the epitaph-self. The concept stopped me in my tracks, as it was a brilliant (and somewhat chilling) illustration of two facets of a person—their achievements and goals (resume-self) versus their values and relationships (epitaph-self). Here's my brief take of his framework:

An epitaph is a phrase or statement that's written to memorialize someone; the sort of thing that's said about someone at a funeral or written on a gravestone. Epitaphs are usually concerned with timeless truths about a person: who the world knew them to be. It's a snapshot of their character.

A resume (or these days, a LinkedIn profile) is the way we present ourselves in professional settings. What have I achieved? What have I done? What's my job title? What are my career accomplishments and ambitions?

Today, many people focus more on their resume-self than their epitaph-self.

Does what you've done define who you are? Or are your character and your values who you are?

Epitaphs often focus on relationships—your friendships, family and community connections. There's not much room for these on your resume. The epitaph is the more human side of who you are. Many hours of our day, however, are spent with the resume-self.

When setting a Goal, it's important to consider the Goal in the context of both selves.

REFLECTION STOP POINT:

× Look at your resume. What are you most proud of and why?

× What resume accomplishments surprise you?

× What are your skills?

× What do you enjoy doing professionally?

× What do you enjoy doing that is not mentioned on your resume?

× How would you write your epitaph today?

× How would you like to be described in your epitaph after you die?

× Is there a difference between your last two answers? What do you need to do to bridge the gap?

× What did you care most about during the last decade? What about the decade before? (and so on)

× What will be important to you in this next decade?

SMART GOAL SETTING

Now it's time to return to your original Goal, the reason you picked up this book in the first place, and take it to the next level.

If you haven't heard of SMART goal setting, you're in for a treat. If you've done SMART goal setting before, you know just how powerful it can be. SMART is an acronym. It stands for Specific, Measurable, Attainable, Relevant, and Time-bound.

A **specific** Goal is clear, meaning that it states your objective in simple and plain language. "I want to leave my job." "I want to find a new house, sign a lease, and move in." "I want to become pregnant."

A **measurable** Goal is quantifiable, and you'll know if you've done it or not. Instead of trying to "lose weight," vow to lose twenty pounds. That way, you will be able to measure your progress. Are you halfway there? Less than halfway? Did you totally kill it and overdeliver on your Goal?

This may seem incompatible with some Goals; how would you measure your progress toward achieving spiritual happiness? Or making a house a home? Yes, even an esoteric Goal can be broken down into milestones. For example, in my personal life, I once had an urgent Goal to feel part of a new community. I had just moved to the suburbs, I was a new mother, and I was feeling adrift.

I broke the big Goal (feel a part of a community) into measurable components: Reach out to three new women this month and invite them to do something socially. Set up one playdate a week. Find a gym or yoga place, and do trial weeks until I commit to one.

When a Goal is measurable, you'll know when you've achieved it.

An **attainable** Goal is something that will stretch you (as any worthwhile Goal does) and is still within your powers. Do you have the skills, knowledge, and ability to make it happen? If so, great. If not, perhaps obtaining said qualifications could be a more appropriate Goal right now.

For example, you might have a Goal of getting married. If you're single, that Goal might feel less attainable. Even so, there are ways to give yourself the tools to make this within your powers. There is a great TED talk from author Amy Webb, who used statistical analysis to find a partner and beat the online dating system. With a little ingenuity, she made a seemingly unobtainable Goal well within her powers.

If you want to climb the Himalayas, you could do it if you planned it right. Lots of people do. Just because it's attainable doesn't mean it will be easy.

A **relevant** Goal is something that is so meaningful and valuable to you that you're willing to put in the time and effort it will take to do it. It's something that might make you feel nervous excitement when you think about it. A Goal without relevance, one that doesn't get you excited, will probably never be reached.

Many people *want* to run a marathon, even if not everyone who wants to actually *does* it. In the last few decades it's become popular to connect the goal of running a marathon to a charitable cause. If you run it to raise money for breast cancer in honor of a dear aunt who was recently diagnosed, that goal will become very relevant and you'll have a much better chance of reaching it even though it isn't easy.

A **time-bound** Goal has a time limit attached to it. This adds a sense of urgency that will help motivate you to get right to work. For example, your Goal might be to run the famous Boston Marathon. The Boston Marathon is held every year on a specific day in April. To be a participating runner, you have to qualify for it by a certain deadline—so those dates would become your built-in timeline.

ACTION STOP POINT: **CREATE YOUR SMART GOAL**

Refer to the original Goal you wrote down in the intro (p. 1). Check the following:

× Is it Specific? Is this a clearly and simply stated Goal? Does it explain what will be accomplished?

× Is it Measurable? How will you know when the Goal has been reached?

× Is it Achievable? Is it possible? Do you have the skills and tools to do it? If not, how do you plan on obtaining those skills and tools?

× Why is it Relevant to you right now? What's the meaning, or purpose, of this Goal and why is it important to you?

× Is it Time-bound? When will you achieve this Goal? Is there a strong enough sense of urgency?

× Rewrite your original Goal so that it's a SMART Goal and meets the above criteria.

REALISTIC GOAL SETTING WITHIN THE PERSONAL (R)EVOLUTION TIMEFRAME

This book is designed for the pursuit and achievement of a Goal in a three-month period. Three months is a significant period of time for change; it's one season in the year, one fiscal quarter, one school term. It's enough time to accomplish quite a bit, and not enough time to get complacent.

When it comes to considering your Goal's timeframe, keep in mind that certain Goals will take longer than others.

For example, if you have a fifteen- or twenty-year career, and your Goal is to find a new career, that's a six-month Goal. If it's your first job, you're currently unemployed and can put *all* your energy into finding a new job, that's a three-month Goal.

So if you have a six-month Goal of finding a new career, for instance, break that down into a smaller Goal of identifying and pursuing possible career paths. Identify what you want and don't want: where the ideal job is located, what kind of company might you work for, what kind of positions you want to target. Determine the who, what, where, when, and how of your Goal. Perhaps your first few months are spent doing research and gathering data.

If your Goal is to have a baby or get married, the timeframe will be dependent on where you are in your life. If you have a partner who is also ready and willing to have a child, then we're down to question of fertility logistics. If you want to get married, and you're single, that's different from someone who wants to get married and has been seriously dating their partner for two years.

Each Goal is achievable. For the purposes of this book, try to find a Goal that is realistically achievable within a three-month timeframe.

VISUALIZATION—MAKE YOUR GOAL FEEL REAL

Studies show that visualization is an important tool to help you achieve the Goal you set. Golfers and Olympic athletes have used this technique for years. In a study by Richard Suinn, a sports psychologist, skiers were monitored by an EMG machine (which detects muscle activity) while they pictured themselves skiing down a slope. Despite the fact that they were only imagining themselves skiing, the EMG results showed that they were activating the same muscles they would use performing the actual activity.

Visualization is shown to:

› Activate the muscles needed for a particular action
› Set up the mind and muscles before you execute, which increases confidence

› Promote calm and relaxation
› Switch your focus to expecting positive outcomes instead of negative
› Help with recovery after an injury
› Promote concentration

The most powerful point on this list for your purposes is "switch your focus to expecting positive outcomes instead of negative". Now there's something to practice. And since you're going after a big, meaty goal, concentration, calm and relaxation will also be good for you.

Visualization will help you to establish your Goal as real. The better you can imagine it, and get your brain to see it, the more likely you are to believe in it and achieve it.

ACTION STOP POINT

× Picture what it will be like when you achieve your Goal: what will it feel like when you do it?

× Live it slowly, experience it, and let this be a detailed experience.

× What will you do to get to that place where you make it happen?

× Who will you be with when it happens?

× Where will you be? How will you celebrate?

× Who will you share the good news with?

× What will it feel like when you do it? How will your life be different?

    × When you look back on how you did it, who helped you?

Let's say your Goal is to complete a book proposal in the next three months. The more you flesh that out, the better. How many words will you write each day? Who will read the proposal during the three months? Where will you sit when you do your writing? Is there anything you need to give up to make space for your writing? During which hours will you work most effectively?

Picturing yourself moving toward your Goal is effective for gaining motivation and preparing yourself for the work it will take to achieve your Goal.

Let's try another example. Let's say you want to conceive a child. And you know you have challenges with fertility. A fertility specialist may ask you to visualize yourself with your baby. What does it feel like to have her in your arms? What is your partner saying? What's an "ordinary" moment at two o'clock on a Sunday afternoon? What's it like bathing your baby? Does she have a favorite blanket or hat? By making that baby tangible, it helps you believe that this can happen.

When you started this chapter, you had a Goal in mind. Through SMART goal setting, you drilled down to get more clear about the hows, whys, and whats, until you had a very specific, clear, achievable picture of yourself achieving the Goal.

And now, with visualization, you're painting a picture and telling a story. You're attaching emotions to the Goal to increase your commitment. The Goal is becoming real for you. This will give you momentum and an emotional connection to the Goal that will help you overcome any challenges you encounter as you pursue it.

SMART goal setting is the planning. Visualizing provides the emotion and momentum that will help you overcome the obstacles you will encounter along the way.

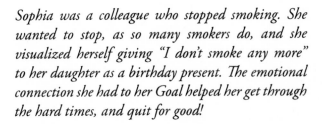

Sophia was a colleague who stopped smoking. She wanted to stop, as so many smokers do, and she visualized herself giving "I don't smoke any more" to her daughter as a birthday present. The emotional connection she had to her Goal helped her get through the hard times, and quit for good!

INSIGHTS AND ACTIONS

As described in the introduction, Insights & Actions is a recurring section at the end of every chapter.

Insights are the thoughts you're thinking now, exciting ideas that are buzzing around in your head. Maybe it's a new thought that you didn't have before this chapter, or maybe it's something you had been thinking about that has new importance or urgency.

Make a careful note of these new thoughts and write them down. If you underlined anything in this chapter, or wrote something in the margin, that's an Insight!

INSIGHTS

(write them here):

1.

2.

3. ....

   ....

4. ....

   ....

5. ....

   ....

ACTIONS

Actions are the next steps you'd like to take toward your Goal. Since your Goal is unique to you, these are primarily assigned by you to you.

In this chapter you already:

› Clarified and confirmed your SMART Goal.
› Reinforced your Goal with a visualization practice. (Spend at least ten minutes picturing yourself achieving the Goal. You can do this once, or you can do this daily; it's up to you. If you want to continue to visualize, put it on your Actions list below.)

Now that you've established your Goal, what are three to five Actions you'd like to take toward achieving it? While answering the questions in the book, did you gain clarity on specific Actions you'd like to take? List them here:

1. ....

   ....

2. ....

   ....

3. ....

   ....

4. ....

....

5. ....

....

Keep in mind that if an action item is on your list two chapters in a row and it's not getting done, you can't list it a third time. You'll need to face the fact that it's not getting done, and either break it down into smaller components or ask yourself *why* it isn't getting done. Is it still important to you? Why or why not?

PREP SHEET

Please complete the following questions before you begin the next chapter:

MY GOAL IS:

....

....

WHERE AM I, ON A SCALE OF 1 TO 10, TOWARD ACHIEVING MY GOAL?

◆───→

   1   2   3   4   5   6   7   8   9   10

WHAT HAVE I ACCOMPLISHED SINCE I BEGAN READING CHAPTER 1?

....

....

WHAT DIDN'T I GET DONE, BUT INTENDED TO DO?

....

....

WHAT OPPORTUNITIES ARE AVAILABLE TO ME RIGHT NOW?

....

....

BY THE END OF THE NEXT CHAPTER I WANT TO:

....

....

ANY INSIGHTS OR NEW AWARENESS THAT EXCITES ME?

....

....

TWO

YOUR GOAL IN THE CONTEXT OF YOUR LIFE: THE WHOLE LIFE MODEL

THE GOAL IN THE CONTEXT OF YOUR LIFE:

THE WHOLE LIFE MODEL

Now that you've set a **SMART** Goal, started visualizing what your future life would be like as you move toward your Goal, and begun taking Actions toward it, it's time to take a look at your life today.

In this chapter, you're going to delve deeper into all the areas of your life with a tool called the Whole Life Model. By looking at the ten key areas of your life, you will have a more in-depth, personalized context to examine what assets you have—including some you may not have realized.

This is the time to pressure test the foundation of your life. Before building an extension on your house, you'd want to make sure the house can handle the extra weight. In the Whole Life Model, you're going to push on the things that hold you together. If your Goal is to have a baby and your marriage isn't strong, let's work on that. If you're working toward a promotion at your health care company and can't stop thinking about your dream of becoming a minister, well, let's address that dream.

At this point, it is not unusual to experience a little hesitation. Clients ask themselves, "Am I *sure* I want to do this?" Or, you may have listed your Actions in the last chapter with great enthusiasm only to find you didn't get them done.

So let's flip that question on its head. Time travel with me, if you will, five years into your future.

REFLECTION STOP POINT

× It's your *Sliding Doors* moment: What does your life look like in five years if you pursue and achieve this Goal?

× What does your life look like if you don't pursue or achieve this Goal? What does *not* "doing this thing you've always wanted to do" look like?

× How has pursuing this changed your life?

This is also a terrific time to review your prep sheet from the end of last chapter. Were there items on your to-do list that you didn't get done? Why didn't you get them done? (Note: This is not a scold, this is a real question. Did you get stuck? Did you feel like it wasn't relevant?) Is there something else you'd like to do instead?

Similarly, what were you able to get done? Why? What is valuable to you in those observations?

FIGURING IT OUT

By the end of this chapter you will have a solid commitment to your Goal. The goal setting and confirmation takes a while (one-fifth of the book!), and I'm an impatient person, so I wouldn't spend time on this unless it was absolutely necessary. I like the old adage "fail to plan and plan to fail." The largest section of this book (first two chapters and intro) is about setting the right target so that the rest of the book flows smoothly—almost effortlessly—and you make that Goal yours.

For reasons I'm not entirely clear on, in the United States we emphasize making an early commitment to a goal and sticking with that goal, despite the fact that a longer evaluation and fact-finding mission may be more appropriate. We ask high school freshmen to pick courses in high school based on the college they want to get into, based on what they want to do in life. Which means we're kind of asking fourteen-year-olds to decide what they want to do with their lives when all they've done is be a child and a student. Seems like a great way to make an uninformed decision!

By the time that fourteen-year-old is thirty, there will be new industries and jobs that they never could have predicted. I worked in the dotcom industry when I was twenty-three; that didn't exist when I was fourteen. Life coaching didn't start until the 1990s; it didn't exist when I was in high school. When today's thirty-somethings were in high school, only criminals were involved in the drug trade—and now marijuana growth and distribution is a large, profitable industry that is legal in many parts of the country.

What would happen if we used high school and college and the better part of our twenties to try on different possibilities, different careers? Why do we need to be decisive before we have any experience in the world?

I see young adults every day who are in their twenties, back at home with their parents after college, and they feel just terrible because they haven't figured it out yet.

Figured it out? After one of those clients leaves my office, the next client will be a fifty-year-old man who thought he had it figured out, went down the predictable and dependable path into law, or journalism, or medicine, and then the path stopped working for him.

There is no "figuring it out." As soon as you've got it figured out, it changes. Or you change. *That* you can be certain of. You have a baby, a marriage, a divorce, an illness, win the lottery. You are constantly in motion; the only thing to figure out is your own ability to evolve as your life and the world evolves. **The only thing that's constant is change.**

As for the kids who don't know what they want to do in high school? Those who are brave enough to admit they don't know? To me, that questioning is the answer. Recognizing what you don't know is a powerful thing—and probably part of why the idea of taking a gap year between high school and college is catching on so fast.

The Culinary Institute of America (C.I.A.), the biggest and most prestigious culinary school in the United States, has a policy that every student must work for six months in a restaurant before they can start culinary school.

Culinary school is awesome; you play with food all day. Working in a restaurant is hard work. Instead of teaching students about food, leaving them with $50,000 of culinary school debt and access to an industry that starts at minimum wage (and doesn't climb much higher), the C.I.A. wants to make sure you desperately want it first.

Requiring time in a restaurant is the ultimate weed-out policy, and I think it's brilliant. Could you imagine if we had the same prerequisite for law school students? Because the goal of culinary school is not to have fun in culinary school, it's to prepare you for a professional life in the food industry. If you don't want to do the latter, you probably want to avoid the former (and the debt that goes with it).

Just as the C.I.A.'s process allows young food enthusiasts to realize whether they truly want to have a culinary career, the Whole Life Model helps you identify the tools you have to pursue your Goal, and confirms that you're ready to pursue this Goal. Or not. If not, you'll pinpoint the areas that you might want to improve before you can realistically pursue this Goal. Once you've done that, you can turn back to Chapter 1 and reset your Goal.

YOUR GOAL IN THE CONTEXT OF YOUR LIFE

x ⊷————————→ •

Ava came to me to help her find a new job, as she had been laid off the prior year. That was our main focus. However, early on in our work together, she revealed that she was forty and seriously dating a terrific guy, and having a baby with him was important to her.

So that became a Goal. An important Goal, in fact—something that Ava wanted to address straight away, given that she was forty and had a medical condition that might make pregnancy complicated. She needed to determine:
   1. Did her partner want a child as well?
   2. What did she need to do to get her body ready for a baby?

• ⊷————————→ ＊

I think it's safe to say that when she made the appointment with a career coach she wasn't thinking she'd walk out looking to make an appointment with a fertility expert.

Since I'm a career and life coach, you get it all—just like Ava did. I believe that your career is just one aspect of a fulfilling life. It's a big part. It's not the whole thing. No matter what your Goal is, setting it within the context of your life helps you to confirm and validate the "it."

THE WHOLE LIFE MODEL

The Whole Life Model is one of the most popular coaching assessment tools. In this chapter, you will use the Whole Life Model to review a series of categories in your life, specifically: health, spirituality, friends, family, love/partnership, personal development, fun and creativity, physical environment, finances, and career.

Using the Whole Life Model, you'll identify what's going well—and what's going *less* well—in your life, based on your level of "satisfaction" and "importance" in the different areas. As you review your life, there are often surprises—things that have been bothering you that you didn't realize you were ignoring, and things worth celebrating that you've been taking for granted.

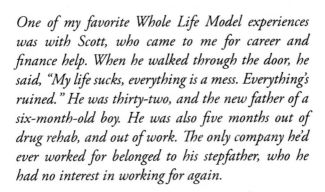

One of my favorite Whole Life Model experiences was with Scott, who came to me for career and finance help. When he walked through the door, he said, "My life sucks, everything is a mess. Everything's ruined." He was thirty-two, and the new father of a six-month-old boy. He was also five months out of drug rehab, and out of work. The only company he'd ever worked for belonged to his stepfather, who he had no interest in working for again.

During his second session, we worked through the Whole Life Model, and found that all the areas of his life were going great, except for career and finance (which are obviously linked). He loved his partner, who he'd been with since he was eighteen. He loved his condo, he had amazing friends from childhood, and had recently started running again. He had a strong relationship with his father and mother. Everything in his life didn't suck. Most of it was pretty awesome.

After we completed the exercise, I said, "I can see what you mean. Your life is not in a good place." He yelled back at me, "What are you talking about? My life is amazing. Have you heard anything I said? My life is pretty great."

And then he caught himself. "You tricked me! You made me say that."

I smiled. Nothing more needed to be said. I hadn't tricked him at all; he just recognized, for himself, all that he had going for him, and chose to focus on that instead of what wasn't working.

Why bring so much attention to your strengths? **Because your strengths are resources you will leverage to help you reach your Goal.**

Scott used his strengths and successes to create energy for the bigger changes he wanted to make. When he felt deflated, we used the Whole Life Model to remind him: "You're a guy who has an incredible relationship with a long-term partner. You've produced a baby and love being a dad. You have solid relationships from childhood." When he talked about his strengths, he realized how skilled and accomplished he was.

● ⇢——————→ ✳

In helping Scott meet his Goal of finding a job, I wanted to bring his attention to the resources he already had. He wanted to find a job and had a huge social network, which is a major advantage. And in fact, that network helped him find a job just two months after we began our work together.

GET TO BASELINE

As you work through the Whole Life Model and observe your strengths, you may also notice things that aren't working as well as you'd like them to; areas that may be preventing you from pursuing your Goal with fluidity and momentum. Those areas will need to be addressed as well.

One of the key categories in the Whole Life Model is health, both physical and mental. This category is of the utmost importance. If your health isn't at baseline—if you aren't sleeping or in a good mental place—then you simply aren't as well equipped as you could be to pursue your Goal. So let's address this one first to determine what you need.

REFLECTION STOP POINT

Here are some of the questions I ask my clients to confirm that they are at baseline with their current state of health:

SLEEP:

× Are you getting enough sleep (eight hours per night)?

× If not, do you keep your phone or other screens in your bedroom?

× When do you shut off media before you go to sleep? Can you close all media thirty to sixty minutes before bed?

× Do you consume caffeine in the afternoon?

× How could you reshape your day to get the full eight hours of sleep that you need?

× What would you need to do to make your bedroom a dark, comfortable, highly optimized sleeping space?

× Do you have a practice for helping calm your mind down when you want to sleep?

EXCERCISE:

× Are you dancing or running or skiing or biking or hiking? What do you do that gets your blood pumping?

× Are you elevating your heart rate three days a week?

× Is there strength training in your life? (That means an activity where you're carrying weight, even your own body weight. It's not just pumping iron, it's walking up hills or stairs.)

EATING:

× Do you have healthy food in the house?

× Are you happy with your eating habits?

× Are you at a healthy weight?

REST & RESTORATION:

× What do you do for fun?

× How do you relax?

× Do you meditate or do yoga? Do you want to?

× Do you have adequate support in the home? If you're a parent, do you have someone who helps with your children? A spouse or romantic partner, or nanny or babysitter?

× Are you doing it all yourself? Do you feel frazzled and overwhelmed because of housekeeping, cooking, and cleaning?

HOW TO PUT MORE HOURS IN YOUR DAY: OUTSOURCE

Asking yourself these questions will help you figure out what *isn't* working for you. You can then decide how to deal with these areas of your life, rather than continuing to struggle with them for no gain. Outsourcing tasks that bring you down, if you can, is a great way to give back some time to yourself that you can spend working on your Goal.

I know so many women (yes, it's most frequently women who bring up this concern) who hate cleaning their house and don't have help. If you have the resources to hire a housekeeper and you're feeling held back by all the cooking and cleaning, by all means—outsource that work.

Sometimes you have to buy back your time so you can use it on things that are of more value to you. If you find yourself saying, "I just don't have enough time," you might try asking yourself how you can buy back your time.

In my office, I've seen a lot of women, particularly working moms, stressing themselves out thinking that they can do it all and can have it all. That's a dangerous mindset. I meet exhausted and depressed people every day who have bought into that mindset and it's not working.

The notion of "having it all" is crazy-making. I subscribe to a different philosophy: "You can have it all, just not all at the same time." So let's prioritize what you'd like to have first.

Part of effective goal prioritizing is figuring out what's not working for you, what you're tolerating, and actively looking for ways to improve the situation. If laundry is piling up, becoming a problem, and holding you back from other things, consider a laundry service. There are some very reasonable services available, and if that's what it takes to save your marriage or your sanity, go for it! If scrubbing toilets wrecks your day, consider a housekeeper or cleaning service. If your sleep, fitness, diet, or time management is out of whack, there are very accessible ways to address those issues. How much junk food do you eat? How much caffeine do you consume? What would a healthier version of yourself look like?

REFLECTION STOP POINT

× Now that you've reflected on your health, specifically your sleeping, eating, exercise, and rest patterns, what do you notice? What is working, and what would you like to bolster?

× What does a healthy version of you look like? Where is the gap between where you are today and where you'd like to be?

WHAT DO YOU VALUE?

In the previous chapter, we discussed the epitaph-self and the resume-self. Although your Goal may be part of your resume-self, your values are your epitaph-self. Where does your Goal fit in with your values? In order for you to obtain your Goal, we want to plant it in fertile soil. Your values are the richest soil there is.

Your values are the ideas you believe in. The actions you take. They are reflected in what (and who) you stand up for, what you consider important. After your basic animal needs are met, what else do you need, and where do you put your efforts?

Sometimes there's a part of your life that you don't value, and you pay little attention to it—health, for example. Then something happens, and you return your attention to this aspect of your life with heightened vigilance. You start to value and take care of your health like never before.

The Whole Life Model will help you identify and reinforce what you value, and what is important to you today.

Connecting your values to your Goal will help you refine and reconfirm your Goal. If your life doesn't accommodate your original Goal, adjust the Goal. You don't adjust your values; they are the foundation you build yourself (and therefore your Goal) upon.

REFLECTION STOP POINT

x Have you ever not been able to do something important because it was eclipsed by something more urgent? (Cancelling a work obligation due to a snowstorm or sick child comes to mind.) What happened as a result of that shifting of obligations?

x In your life, what comes first? Who comes first?

x What's something you outgrew in the last year? Clothes or shoes? People? Habits? A car? Music?

✕ Do you support any causes? March or take a political
   stand? Is there someone, or something that you stood
   up for recently?

✕ At the end of the last chapter, you prepared an Action
   list. What was on your Action list that didn't get done?
   Why not?

THE WHOLE LIFE MODEL: LET'S DO THIS

In the previous section, we explored the idea that a Goal
can shift based on an awareness of values. I hope the open-
ended questions were thought provoking and provided
some Insights.

You are now ready to sharpen that focus. The Whole Life
Model will help you take inventory of ten areas of your life
as they are today, and your general state of satisfaction with
those areas.

Before we begin, please reconnect with the **SMART** Goal
you formed in the previous chapter. Write it here:

Great! Still looking good, or do you have any reservations?
Or perhaps a little of both? In the space below, state why:

Many people start planning their gardens by daydreaming
about the kinds of flowers and plants they want (or coveting
their neighbor's bounty). Then there's that moment where
the gardener takes a look at their own space. What kind of
light is there? What is the soil like? What kind of weather is

expected in the region? What's already growing there? How much space is there? The gardener adjusts his dreams based on the reality of the space. As much as I love palm trees, it's unlikely that I will grow them in my backyard in New Jersey.

This chapter is that moment. We've got the SMART Goal we've daydream-believed in; now it's time to walk into your backyard and see what you've got to work with and refine your Goal within the context of your assets and values today.

If I want a palm tree *that* badly, perhaps the answer is a move to Florida. Or California. So I'll need to plan for that move before I can plant the tree.

This exercise will ensure you can and will achieve the Goal you've selected, that this is the best Goal for you right now. This will help you commit to your change, and you'll start to increase your investment and motivation.

Using the Whole Life Model, you will review a series of categories: health, spirituality, friends, family, love/partnership, personal development, fun and creativity, physical environment, finances, and career.

Then you will rank each of these categories on a scale of 1 to 10 based on two scales:

1. Your **satisfaction** with this area of your life *at present*
2. The **importance** of this area of your life to you *at present*. Those that you rank as most important are what you value most.

After you score yourself, please provide the deviation, which is the importance score minus the satisfaction score. In some cases, you will have a negative number.

Here is a more in-depth explanation of each of the ten areas. After each explanation, take a moment and scale yourself on each of the two parameters: satisfaction and importance. Then, take a few moments to explain the rationale for your scaling.

HEALTH

This area refers to your physical and mental health. (You've already done some work in this area in the previous pages.) Are you content with your level of fitness and exercise? Do you consider yourself healthy? If not, are you receiving the medical care you need? Do you sleep and eat right? Do you have health insurance so you can get care if you need it?

Are you mentally OK? Do you consider yourself at or above baseline, or do you need some help to get to baseline? Do you see a therapist, or would you like to? Are you taking medication, and is that working for you? Do you think you need to increase or reduce your medication?

On a scale of 1 to 10:

I am satisfied with my physical and mental health: ___

This area of life is important to me: ___

Importance minus satisfaction: ___

Explanation:

SPIRITUALITY

In this book, spirituality refers to your spirit and your place in the larger scheme of things; the ways that you are connected to other people, beings, thoughts, or nature. It's how you connect with the world at large, a larger sense of belonging, peace, and life. Some people tend to their spirituality with a regular yoga or meditation practice. Others go to church every Sunday, birdwatch, or volunteer regularly.

On a scale of 1 to 10:

I am satisfied with my spirituality: ___

This area of life is important to me: ___
Importance minus satisfaction: ___
Explanation:

FRIENDS

You don't need a huge network of friends to feel a sense of satisfaction here. Do you have a couple of friends who you can turn to when you want to connect? Are you satisfied with these relationships? Who do you have in your life who knows your story and thinks you're terrific? Do you see these people with a frequency that's satisfying to you? Do you have work friends, high school friends, college friends, friendships you've nurtured throughout your life? Who is your newest friend? Are you able to shed the friends you've outgrown?

On a scale of 1 to 10:

I am satisfied with my friendships: ___
This area of life is important to me: ___
Importance minus satisfaction: ___
Explanation:

FAMILY

Family can refer to your family of origin, your current family, or both, depending on what's important to you right now. How are your relationships with your parents? Your children? Do you want and have children? Do your parents need support, and are they able to get it? How are your relationships with your siblings? Do you want to improve them and can you?

On a scale of 1 to 10:

I am satisfied with my family: ___

This area of life is important to me: ___

Importance minus satisfaction: ___

Explanation:

LOVE/PARTNERSHIP

This refers to your primary relationship. Do you have one? If not, is that okay with you, or do you want to find a partner? For some people, this might not refer to a spouse—it could be a best friend, someone who looks out for them, a witness to their life. Others might be happily single.

On a scale of 1 to 10:

I am satisfied with my love/partnership:___

This area of life is important to me:___

Importance minus satisfaction: ___

Explanation:

PERSONAL DEVELOPMENT

According to Daniel Pink, author of *Drive: The Surprising Truth About What Motivates Us*, one of the key components of satisfying work is working toward mastery in an area where mastery is achievable (more about this in Chapter 6). Are you working toward mastery in an area? My local postman is also a triathlete; his job is a satisfying way for him to earn a living, and his need for personal development is sated by his hobby.

Some corporations focus on providing growth opportunities like leadership training or management development for their employees, which helps their staff gain mastery in a way that ultimately helps the corporation. How are you developing, personally, and moving your mastery forward? This may be as simple as reading novels, or as complex as learning a new language.

On a scale of 1 to 10:

I am satisfied with my personal development:_____

This area of life is important to me:_____

Importance minus satisfaction: _____

Explanation:

FUN & CREATIVITY

A fun, creative outlet is something you do for the sake of doing it. This could mean playing an instrument, making a bonfire, taking an adult cooking class, playing charades, or watching stand-up comedy. It could mean dancing in your living room or dressing up for a costume party. It's active. Many clients overlook this area or see it as frivolous, rather than recognizing that fun and creativity is an opportunity to recharge. Courts in the Middle Ages had their jesters; every major television network has its late-night comedy shows. Everyone needs to have some fun and an opportunity to create and contribute.

On a scale of 1 to 10:

I am satisfied with the fun and creativity in my life:_____

This area of life is important to me:_____

Importance minus satisfaction: _____
Explanation:

PHYSICAL ENVIRONMENT

When you think about the physical spaces you inhabit—your home, your car, your office—how do these spaces impact you? Do they add to your calm, peace, and inspiration? Or are they cluttered and burdensome? One of my clients refers to a person's physical environment as your "third skin" (first is your actual skin and second is your clothes). How do the spaces you inhabit contribute to your well-being? Are they good for you or not? What do you need to do to improve them?

On a scale of 1 to 10:

I am satisfied with my physical environment:_____

This area of life is important to me:_____

Importance minus satisfaction: _____

Explanation:

FINANCES

Are you comfortable with your money, or are you in debt? The majority of adults, especially those coming out of college, are deeply in debt and, unfortunately, many don't know how to deal with it or have chosen not to deal with it.

Now is the time to take a good long look at your finances; where they are and where you want them to be. Are you on track? Deep in debt? Have extra money? Do you have a trust fund and are you stressed about the possibility of losing it? Are you realistic about spending the money you have? Do you consider yourself financially healthy?

On a scale of 1 to 10:

I am satisfied with my finances:____

This area of life is important to me:____

Importance minus satisfaction: ____

Explanation:

CAREER

Since I'm a career and life coach, most of my clients come to me to talk about career; this is the one issue they know they want to work on. I find that people are willing to invest time and money in addressing their career needs. In fact, your career may be the reason you picked up this book in the first place.

Is your career satisfying? Does your career satisfy your need to earn a living? Does your career satisfy your desire to contribute to society in a meaningful way? Do you feel appreciated in your workplace? Are you able to do your work the way you'd like to? Does your job make use of your skills and talents? Can you see a path to continued job growth?

On a scale of 1 to 10:

I am satisfied with my career:____

This area of life is important to me:____

Importance minus satisfaction: ____

Explanation:

THE WHOLE IS MORE IMPORTANT THAN THE PARTS

You have committed to this book for a reason. It may be that you want a better relationship or a different career, or to figure out how to manage your life now that you have a baby.

The Whole Life Model is useful because it puts the importance of any one area of life (career, finances, family) in the context of the rest of your life. The solution to a challenge in any one area becomes more evident when seen through the lens of your larger life.

x ↔——————→ •

My husband, Aaron, made an enormous career change after a successful twenty-five-year career. And he was only able to do it because he reconceived his career within the context of the rest of his life. He had been a journalist for twenty-five years, working for companies like The Street.com, Yahoo Finance, and Fortune, where he had been Editor-in-Chief and on-camera host for the last decade. He led teams of fifteen to fifty people and was well regarded by his colleagues.

And yet he came to a point where he realized that the profession he found so meaningful was no longer a fit for his lifestyle needs. As a father of four, with three of those children under age five, he recognized that compensation in journalism has stagnated, and seasoned journalists, editors, and managers were being replaced by two or three hungry young journalists willing to work for less. Plus, for the top journalism jobs, he would need to commute at least two hours every day, which made it difficult to be as involved as he wanted to be with his family and community.

I cannot understate the significance of this shift. Journalism is a calling, and his identity was as a journalist. Because he knew that career could no longer satisfy several sections of his Whole Life, including his physical environment (i.e. commute), family, partnership, and finance, he was able to ask a different question and set a different SMART Goal: How could he use his writing, editing, and team management skills in a different way? He needed his job to give him the opportunity to be around for his four children, raise his income, and reduce his commute. That's very different than looking for another Editor-in-Chief job in New York City.

He left journalism and moved to a corporate career. He uses his editorial and management skills and is working for a successful, growing, global company. He has a far better work/life balance and has a leadership role in a growing industry. Plus, he gets to drop his kids off at school and attend their mid-day events—something he never would have been able to do otherwise.

Aaron's current career isn't the path he originally built or envisioned, and it enables him to have the life he wanted to have. He redefined career "success" in light of the life he wanted to have.

Incidentally, it was this very coaching process that led my husband to make that decision. He was coaching-curious, and I suggested he try a session with me. I treated him like any other client; he scheduled an appointment, waited in my waiting room, and did his prep sheet like everyone else. I did my best to un-know what I knew about his situation so that I could listen to him talk about his wants and needs with fresh coaching ears.

You can make a "good" career move that gets you more money or a better title. Or you can consult with your friendly, neighborhood career and life coach (me!), who will help you establish and pursue a Goal that aligns with the entirety of your life, not just one area.

BACK TO YOUR WHOLE LIFE MODEL

You've scaled yourself for significance and importance in each of the ten areas of the Whole Life Model, explored the rationale for your choices, and found your deviation. Well done! Now let's interpret the results to determine which of these areas are doing well, and which you may want to focus your attention on.

The first thing I'd like to do is clarify which of the areas of your life are most **important** to you. Those are the areas that you ranked between seven and ten. These are key. Which three areas did you rank highest? Please write them in the space below.

Next, look at your deviation and find the number pairs with the biggest gap or difference between them. If finance satisfaction is at a 2 and importance is an 8, that's a gap of 6—and that's significant. However, if spirituality satisfaction is at an 8 and the importance is 2, that's a deviation of -10, which means it's not something we need to focus on. In fact, any negative numbers can be disregarded for the purposes of this exercise.

Which three or four areas have the largest deviation value?

The areas of greatest importance are what you value most. Ideally, any action you take at this point will address your need in these areas. The deviations identify where you're experiencing the most significant dissatisfaction and where change is most needed.

This is why many of my clients come to me for help in one area (career change) and leave with an additional Goal (have a baby). Using the Whole Life Model, they recognize another area of great importance that they did not have awareness of prior to completing the exercise.

At this point, you may see that you need to shift your Goal and prioritize a different need. If you want to start finding a new job so that you can leave your husband, and you're not sure if you want to leave your husband, you may want to have two Goals: a job search *and* to begin marital counseling or individual therapy to decide if you're in or out of the relationship.

Ideally, your **SMART** Goal reflects your top deviations. If not, you will need to shift your Goal to address your most acute need. Yes, that means a return to Chapter 1 to create a new **SMART** Goal.

If your Goal aligns with what is important to you and your areas of need, please proceed.

ACTION STOP POINT

- × Which categories of the Whole Life Model are more important to you than you realized?

- × What new Insights do you have about your life after completing the Whole Life Model?

- × How do your values (areas of importance) reinforce your Goal? What is the link?

- × If you are doing very well in areas of high value (both satisfaction and importance ranked above 7), why is that? How can you use these assets as you pursue your Goal?

COMMIT: CONNECT YOUR EMOTION TO YOUR REFINED SMART GOAL

At the end of Chapter 1, you created Insights, then translated those Insights into an Action Plan with a **SMART** Goal. At the conclusion of the chapter, you completed a visualization to help reinforce your Goal.

In this chapter, you've completed the Whole Life Model, a full analysis and assessment of your values, and determined your satisfaction with areas of your life that are more and less important to you. You've determined, once and for all, that your Goal is the right Goal to pursue.

Now, let's reinforce your commitment (ink it, baby!) by confirming that achieving this Goal will change your life:

- › If I achieve this Goal, how will my life be different?
- › What does my life look like when I do this?

› When I achieve this Goal, what will I have that I don't have now? More money? More time? Better health?
› Who is impacted when I achieve this Goal?
› Having achieved this Goal, what would my life be like, in terms of my own satisfaction, on a scale of 1 to 10?
› What will achieving this Goal enable me to do that I can't do at present?

YOUR FINANCIAL HEALTH: BE HONEST

Money can be a subject of anxiety for many people, and financial worries often hold people back from reaching for their Goal. Facing the realities of their money situation can help refine their Goal.

Isabella was a lawyer who ended up staying in her legal career because the more she looked around, the better she seemed to have it. By securing a raise and better work conditions over the course of our work together, the grass no longer seemed as green on the other side. When we concluded our work, she said, "I thought that by hiring a career coach, I'd end up finding out that the perfect career for me was flower arranging or something like that." As it turns out, entry-level flower arrangers make far less than Georgetown lawyers with thirty years of experience.

Although Isabella was willing to take a bit of a salary dip for her dream career, she wasn't willing to cut it as substantially as that alternative career would require.

Alternatively, you may be in a better position to invest in a career change than you realize.

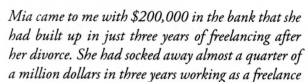

Mia came to me with $200,000 in the bank that she had built up in just three years of freelancing after her divorce. She had socked away almost a quarter of a million dollars in three years working as a freelance stylist. Wow.

She had an idea of her next project—something big that she was passionate about and uniquely skilled to pursue. However, it would be more freelance work. She came to me because she had financial anxiety and wanted help finding a job as soon as possible. When we reviewed her finances (and revealed her ample cushion), she realized that she could reduce the pressure she was putting on herself to earn. I asked, "What if you gave yourself a year to figure out your project and used that money to pay your expenses for the year?" She realized she had what she needed to invest in herself, and she did it.

Money was holding her back because she thought she couldn't afford to pursue one of her most important Goals. She was sitting on a huge asset that could, in fact, enable the pursuit of her Goal.

Of the people I meet for an initial appointment, 75 percent are disconnected with their monthly finances. They don't know how much money they need to pay their bills each month; they operate on a rough estimate, which may be way off, or worse, they operate from a place of debt. They may not have a financial plan or know whether or not they are moving toward their retirement goal. So it's important to get your financial ducks in a row. This is as good a time as any! Just like I like my clients to go to the doctor for an annual checkup, financial awareness can lead to improved financial health, reduced financial anxiety, and empowerment to address what needs to be fixed.

If you recognized that your finances are a little weaker than you'd like them to be, take some time to go over your bank statements and bills, and figure out your monthly expenses. Include housing, food, utilities, transportation, debt repayment, vacations, and all the other areas where you spend money each month. Figure out the exact dollar amount that you need to keep your life running. Identify your "burn rate," and what kind of income you need, at a minimum, to meet your needs.

IS PURSUING YOUR GOAL RIGHT AT THIS TIME?

Before I begin work with a new client, one of the things I try to determine during our conversation is whether or not they are at baseline.

So before you pursue coaching, are there specific obligations, health issues, or other challenges in your life that are preventing you from going deep into the questions presented in this chapter? If you are struggling with the questions asked because they are bringing up negative feelings such as anxiety or depression, or you need to heal or strengthen another area first, now is the time to bring in other professionals, such as therapists or psychiatrists to bring you to baseline first.

Coaching is hard work, and just like an ambitious physical endeavor, you've got to be ready for it before you begin.

ACTION STOP POINT:

× By the end of this chapter, you will be clear on and committed to that one thing you want to work on— committed enough to tell someone else about it, like your friends or your partner.

× Consider this person, or people, as your stakeholders; they're the people who will be affected and impacted, and that's something to work through with them. By sharing your Goal, you'll also be building a network of support and accountability for this project. (More to come on this in Chapter 7.)

I'M BLOCKED, EVEN AFTER THIS

This book isn't your only resource; if you're experiencing a blockage or something isn't working, I can provide even more assistance. You can always reach out to me through my website, http://www.allisontask.com, or set up your own introductory coaching session.

There is one more assessment tool my clients find useful for values clarity: it's called the Via Character Strengths Test, and you can find it at https://www.viacharacter.org. If you're struggling with the Whole Life Model or just feeling unclear about what's important to you, try this tool. It can help.

INSIGHTS AND ACTIONS

INSIGHTS:

› What are your top areas of strength you identified with the Whole Life Model?

> › Is there anything new you need to do before pursuing your **SMART** Goal?
> › Can you do these things easily or will you be shifting your Goal?

Write your new **SMART** (or re-confirmed) Goal here:

Remember, if you underlined anything in this chapter, or wrote something in the margin, that's an Insight. Please capture the key ones here:

1.

2.

3.

4.

5.

ACTIONS:

Who are two to three people who will be impacted by, or who are important to, achieving your Goal? What's the best way to share your Goal with them?

1.

2.

Take a good look at your finances, or schedule a meeting with a financial planner. Will your finances have an impact on your Goal? If you're thinking about changing careers, what's the minimum amount you need to make for the kind of life you're comfortable living?

What are three to five Actions you can take this week to move you toward your Goal?

1.

2.

3.

4.

5.

PREP SHEET

Please complete the following questions before you begin the next chapter:

MY GOAL IS:

WHERE AM I, ON A SCALE OF 1 TO 10, TOWARD ACHIEVING MY GOAL?

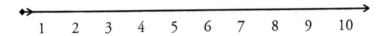

1   2   3   4   5   6   7   8   9   10

WHAT HAVE I ACCOMPLISHED SINCE I BEGAN READING CHAPTER 2?

WHAT DIDN'T I GET DONE, BUT INTENDED TO DO?

WHAT OPPORTUNITIES ARE AVAILABLE TO ME RIGHT NOW?

BY THE END OF THE NEXT CHAPTER I WANT TO:

ANY INSIGHTS OR NEW AWARENESS THAT EXCITES ME?

THREE

C'MON GET HAPPY: PRACTICE HAPPINESS AND GAIN MOMENTUM

C'MON GET HAPPY: PRACTICE HAPPINESS AND GAIN MOMENTUM

x ✦>————————→ ●

If I had to pick just one chapter from this book that could change your life, it's this one. This chapter has simple tools that you can use on a daily basis. Now that you've completed the goal-setting exercises, visualized, committed to, and shared your Goal, I hope that you are feeling confident about it, recognizing that it is within your grasp.

As we move through this chapter, we're going to get into your mental game. Are you in a good place? Are you feeling fired up about what's ahead of you, or are you thinking, "I don't know if I can do this." If the latter is true, that's OK.

In this chapter, I will help you shift the way you look at your Goal by helping you reset your perspective, recognize the assets you have, and believe that the future you want can and will become reality.

WILLPOWER VS. EASE

When I worked in the healthy cooking business, people would ask me how to lose weight. Losing weight too often focuses on loss and its cousin, deprivation. The common philosophy is that in order to lose, you have to give up the foods you want and love. To flip that, I would tell people "Instead of focusing on what you *can't* have let's focus on what you *can* to have before you have the extras. You *can* have dessert (if you'd like), after you drink twelve glasses of water, enjoy nine servings of fruit and vegetables, and exercise for at least thirty minutes." Sometimes, people who are losing weight have cravings because they're depleted, they don't have enough of what they need. So let's deal with depletions like dehydration and hunger, before you can have the presence of mind to manage your cravings.

In other words, let's satisfy your needs before you give into your wants. And if you don't satisfy those needs, the wants can become so loud and desperate they can take over.

You know when you're in a tough situation, like sitting in a car with a bad driver, and you just hold on tight, hoping you'll make it out alive? When you look at your hands, your knuckles are almost white because you're hanging on for dear life. That's what it's like when you rely on willpower to get you through tough situations, and that's a tremendous amount of stress to your system.

Many of my clients have tried—and failed—to reach Goals in the past by relying on willpower, or by "white-knuckling it." It doesn't work for dieting and it doesn't work for achieving Goals.

Think of the impact of that stress. You can't think straight because you're anxious, nervous, frustrated, scared, and relying on willpower. When you are thinking clearly, and have access to your logical brain because you are committed to a clear Goal that's meaningful and in line with your values, you can stay focused on the task at hand without white-knuckling it past temptations.

For example, I want to exercise. So I have a simple exercise routine. I take a class 3 mornings per week, Monday through Friday at 8:30AM. I like the instructors and the other people in the class, and I know it's effective. I don't have to think about it. I just show up, do my exercise, and get on with my day.

If I have to ask myself the question, "Should I exercise today or not?" I'm testing my willpower. If I have to decide whether or not I exercise, if I have that choice, there's the possibility it won't happen.

By asking fewer questions and just showing up, I am better able to reach my fitness Goal and focus my energy on other things.

When it comes to your Goal, the fewer decisions you have to make, the better. Asking too many questions leads to too many decisions, which leads to decision fatigue—and means you'll have less willpower as the day goes on. That's why so many people find themselves cheating on their diet at night after being "good" all day.

So what tools do we have to use instead of willpower? Insights and Actions. Use the Insights to make a decision, use the Action to move forward. Insights lead to Actions. Don't question, just do.

I've heard stories about '50s housewives simplifying their lives by creating a predictable family meal plan: Monday was meatloaf night, Tuesday was pasta night, Wednesday was breaded chicken, and so on. Mundane? Perhaps. But it also kept the family fed without having to reinvent the wheel every week. Without the burden of having to invent new meals that would delight the family, these housewives knew their family would be fed effectively and could focus on other matters.

In addition to staying focused on action throughout this chapter, I also want to demonstrate the invisible power of positive thinking to help you achieve your Goal.

x ↔———————→ •

Emily didn't get her homework done one week because she stayed up until four o'clock in the morning, making apple pie. She wanted to make everything from scratch and wake up to a beautiful apple pie in the morning, which she did. Unfortunately, she also ended up ruining her whole day (and subsequent days) because she was so exhausted from the endeavor. She explained, "I just wanted to have an apple pie day." I responded, "Yeah, but if you have a good night's sleep, every day can be an apple pie day." She liked that. I wrote those words on the board in my office—"Every day can be an apple pie day." It was the most Pollyanna sentence I'd ever written. And it's so true.

• ↔———————→ ✢

We all want apple pie days. And we all know that one person who's always smiling. Maybe it's your yoga instructor, a friend at the coffee shop, or someone you see at the grocery store. They're almost annoyingly blissful—and that's exactly what makes them so awesome. You can't help but feel happy when you're around them.

That's the invisible power of positivity—that person having the superpower of the smile. And this chapter will take you there so that you, too, can have an apple pie day (with a full night of sleep).

ACTION STOP POINT

x   Name three people in your life who are always smiling.

× What might they be doing (or not doing) that makes them so happy?

× When is the last time you had an apple pie day?

× Recall a time when someone commented on how terrific you looked or how happy you seemed. When was it? Why do you think you were giving off that vibe?

THE SCIENCE OF HAPPINESS

Three cheers for Martin Seligman, the father of positive psychology. Before he popularized this movement, the field of psychology generally focused on what was wrong with patients and how to fix broken brains. Seligman, a University of Pennsylvania professor and former president of the American Psychological Association, instead studied what made people feel well. He led psychologists to focus on how the patient can be responsible for her own state of wellness.

Slowly, scientists moved from exclusively studying pathos and aberrant behavior to studying what leads to healthy, long lives. By now you're familiar with the concept that strong relationships and a positive social network are linked to a longer lifespan. As scientists researched the attributes of a healthy mind and a healthy life, they revealed that a positive mindset is linked to physiological changes in the body such as lower cortisol—which is also associated with a reduction of heart disease and leads to longer lifespans. When science is applied to concepts like happiness, positivity, and optimism, we learn the power that we, as individuals, have to ensure we live better lives.

Positive psychology isn't cheerleading, or denying problems. It's not just about positive mantras and asking the universe for what you want. Positive psychology is a field that studies the powerful links between happiness and health (both mental and physical) and personal success and contentment. I like to think of it as the study of how people live terrific lives.

The studies about meditation and monks, and the positive impact that meditation has on your body? That's straight-up positive psychology (along with neuroscience and physiology). The "gorilla study" that studies attention and focus? Positive psychology. (Also worth YouTube-ing.) The multiple studies on aging and the elderly that determines why some people live longer than others, even if they drink a Manhattan at cocktail hour every day? You guessed it, positive psychology.

And of course, the pioneering thinking in the field is central to what I do in my office with clients. My understanding of positive psychology started with classes I took as an undergrad at Cornell University while pursuing my major of human development and family studies. (Each class started with a professor explaining, "No really! This is *real* science." I always wondered why they protested that much. Social scientists, certainly those studying topics like happiness and love, were apparently not getting the respect their biology and chemistry colleagues received.)

I've been influenced by *The Happiness Advantage* by Shawn Achor and *Happier: Learn the Secrets to Daily Joy and Lasting Fulfillment* by Tal Ben-Shahar. These books were based on the popular Harvard happiness class the two men created (Positive Psychology 1504). In 2015, their class became Harvard's most popular course of all time.

Finally, The Greater Good Science Center, which is part of University of California, Berkeley, offers a free online class on happiness through http://edX.org (to further the greater good, naturally). This class provides an overview of the field of positive psychology and the current thinking on happiness.

If this chapter inspires you to learn more, I wholeheartedly recommend a deeper dive into any of these resources.

Here are some highlights from decades of research on positive psychology, along with exercises and Actions that will apply those findings to your own work.

DEMONSTRATING THE CASE FOR HAPPINESS

One of my favorite positive psychology researchers began her research two decades before Seligman's work. Ellen Langer, the first woman in Harvard's psychology department to receive tenure, conducted some legendary creative research. She must have seemed like a mad scientist at the time, researching the power of thought on aging and health.

In 1979, she conducted a simulated time-travel experiment now referred to as "the counter clockwise study." She took eight men in their late 70s to a one-week retreat that had been retrofitted to appear as if it was twenty years earlier. While on retreat, they were encouraged to act as if the past was present—as if it were actually 1959. They were given newspapers from the Eisenhower era and were encouraged to talk about their lives when they were living at that time.

The results were remarkable. The subjects showed a significant improvement in flexibility, posture, and hand strength, and their eyesight and memory both improved by 10%. Strangers were shown photos of the subjects from before and after the experiment and perceived a three-year drop in their ages. After one week!

In another study, Langer's team asked hotel maids how much exercise they got. All replied, "None." The eighty-four maids were then split into two groups. One group was taught that their work of cleaning actually was exercise, while the other group was given no such information. Langer wanted to see if changing their perception of their work as exercise would have an impact on them physically.

Three months after this "lesson," Langer and her team evaluated the maids. The group that had been taught that their work was exercise demonstrated weight loss, lower blood pressure, lower waist-to-hip ratios, and lower BMI.

Langer demonstrated that what we believe our life to be has a direct effect on the physical aging process. By actively practicing happiness and shifting your mindset, you can achieve a positive impact on your health.

Another study showing the importance of being positive is detailed in Shawn Achor's book. Researchers set out to determine whether the happiness of doctors could affect the quality of their diagnoses. A group of doctors was given a set of symptoms to analyze. They were then split into three groups—one was primed to feel happy, the second was given neutral medical statements to read beforehand, and the third control group was given nothing. The purpose of the study was see how fast the physicians arrived at the correct diagnosis and to determine how well they avoided making errors resulting from inflexibility in thinking, known as "anchoring."

The happy doctors made the right diagnosis faster. On average, they came to the correct diagnosis only 20% of the way through the manuscript—nearly twice as fast as the control group.

The most interesting part of the study, however, was how the researchers elicited positive emotions from the doctors. It didn't take a cash reward or the promise of a promotion to boost the doctors' moods and make them more effective. All it took was a small gift of candy right before they started the task. They didn't even get to eat the candy, as the scientists wanted to ensure that the heightened blood sugar levels didn't affect the results. The study proved that even the smallest gestures of positivity can give someone a serious competitive edge.

An important part of maintaining a positive mindset is to reconceive failure as an opportunity for growth. This is what Achor refers to as "falling up." Capitalizing on down moments helps build upward momentum. Say, for example, I'm experiencing a bit of a dip in my coaching business. Rather than desperately chasing more clients, I say, "Well, that's kind of terrific. Now that I've got some extra time, I'm going to sink my feet into learning about new coaching techniques or work on my book." When you fall up, you find a way to take positive advantage of a situation you'd normally perceive of as a setback.

Another idea in Achor's book is the Tetris Effect. Also known as selective perception, this refers to the technique of training your brain to scan the world for possibility and then capitalize on it. (Boy, do I use this with my clients who are looking for a new job!) It's based on a study from the Harvard Department of Psychology, where researchers asked twenty-seven people to play Tetris for multiple hours over three days. For days after they stopped, they reported seeing Tetris shapes everywhere. They'd look at a brick wall and figure out which bricks could fall in between others, or they'd go to Costco and see Tetris shapes in the stacked boxes. This is called a cognitive aftereffect, and it shows how our brain can get stuck in the patterns we practice.

That's a big idea. **Our brain gets stuck in the patterns we practice.** So, knowing that, where's the opportunity to shift our thinking, step away from negative habitual thoughts, and shift them into more positive ones? For example, if you look in the mirror each morning and identify three things you like about yourself, you'll begin to see these qualities more than the so-called flaws you may focus on.

Charlotte had a fantastic network. She freelanced and was interested in finding full-time work. She told me that her friends couldn't believe she couldn't find work. "They keep telling me how capable and talented I am."

When I asked her what she thought, Charlotte had a laundry list of the reasons why she couldn't find work. Her age, her lack of traditional experience, "New York City companies won't even consider me", etc. Instead of focusing on her strengths and assets, she used those moments to tell her friends (and me) how wrong we were. She was putting a great deal of energy into explaining, convincing herself and her friends why she couldn't get a job*. She was investing a great deal of time and energy flipping her assets into limitations. Eek!

This storytelling kept Charlotte stuck. It was time for Charlotte to rewrite her story based on facts.

ACTION STOP POINT

x   Of the positive psychology research mentioned above, what was your favorite study and why?

---

* Less than six months after we began work together, Charlotte had turned down a full time offer, and was in the final round of interviews for two more full time jobs at boutique agencies, one which was based in New York City. In an email describing the opportunity, Charlotte wrote, "I would *love* this job but even if I don't get [this job], it's been such a huge validation of my experience, resume etc."

× Think back to a reunion you've attended (high school, college, or family). Has anyone ever showed up noticeably different in a good way? How did you perceive that they were different? Do you know what caused the change?

× Do you know anyone who healed after a major illness and returned to life with a more positive outlook? Describe in detail who, how, and why.

× Have you ever acted in a certain way to someone in a position to help you (bartender, doctor, police officer, etc.)? Assuming you didn't bribe them or engage in other illegal activity, what did you do to encourage them to help you? How did it work? Were you employing any positive psychology concepts? Which ones?

× Share a story where you had an opportunity to "fall up"—when something negative happened, and you turned lemons into lemonade. What did you do? How did it impact you?

× Selective perception is a concept I shared in the "Tetris Effect" study. Is there something you tell yourself regularly, either negative or positive? What is it?

× Is there something new you want to tell yourself related to your Goal? How can you practice telling yourself this regularly (the way the students practiced Tetris)?

THE "THREE GOOD THINGS" EXERCISE

The best way to train your brain to think positively is by observing positive situations around you—positive experiences that you've had. The positive psychology exercise I "assign" my clients more than any other is called Three Good Things, and it is described in detail on the Greater Good Science Center web site, https://ggia.berkeley.edu/.

Each night before you go to sleep, write down (or thoroughly think through) three good things that happened to you that day. By taking stock of the day you've just inhabited, and picking out the positive highlights from that day, you're engaging in selective perception. By carefully and thoroughly detailing the memory, your brain is re-experiencing the memory you're curating, and with it comes positive feelings and emotions.

Let's say you're recalling the way your best friend's three-year-old daughter scrambled up to sit on your lap and asked you to read her a book. You can remember how you perceived that the child felt safe with you, and how warm the child's body felt in your lap. You can recall her inquisitive expressions as you read the book, or any sweet questions she asked. You can think about the pride you felt as she recited some of the pages by herself, and the gratitude you felt being part of this child's life as she grows. By reliving those feelings, you may actually feel them again, from tingles inside your body to perhaps even shedding a tear of joy! These are real emotions you're bringing back, based on reliving a positive memory.

The more specific and tactile you get with the Three Good Things exercise, the better. For example, maybe you're remembering what it was like to see the sunrise and share it with a bird that sat beside you that morning. Maybe it's that first sip of a coffee you enjoy by yourself in the morning (yes, it can be that ordinary!). By actively reliving the memory, you're accessing more positive feelings about it and making it more real. Remember our visualization exercise in Chapter 1? This is similar.

And that's just one! Spend at least five to ten minutes writing about or thinking about three separate highlights from your day. By taking a moment to relive the best moments of your day, you will feel gratitude and joy for your terrific life.

ACTION STOP POINT

× Practice finding each of your Good Things. Think back over the day and try to remember all the details that helped the moment be special. Say it aloud, write it down or just think it through.

× How did you feel before the good thing happened? What exactly was said? What did the person's face look like when they were sharing that with you?

× If you were playing with an animal, what did its fur feel like on your skin? Was it fuzzy and soft? Shiny? Small and fragile or big and strong?

× Was it raining? Were you wet or super dry? Was it warm? Freezing cold? Warm breeze or refreshing splash in the ocean?

× The more details you use to recreate the moment, the more powerful this gratitude exercise will be.

As you continue this each day, you'll get better at finding your three things, and it will eventually become habit. People often tell me how much this exercise has changed their life. I've had couples who do the exercise together each night and find that it brings them closer. I've had parents tell me it's a family ritual they do every night—and their kids really look forward to sharing. It's one of the few activities you can do each day that instantly makes you feel so much better—so as you practice, you'll find you can't wait to do it!

FINDING AWE

What if nothing good happens to you? Well, obviously I can't agree with the premise, since waking up in the morning is a pretty terrific thing. As is opening your eyes, taking a shower, or having the ability to read this very book. So you can always find something.

There's a second exercise that will heighten your awareness of good things around you. This exercise is called an Awe Walk, and it's also from the Greater Good Science Center. It's very simple. Take yourself to a new place, or be prepared to see a familiar place with fresh eyes. It's best if this place is somewhere in nature: a local park, a pond or stream, a hike. Even a friend's backyard can do the trick. Give yourself some time, thirty minutes to an hour, and take a walk. Observe what you are seeing. Actively look for something new, fresh, unusual, beautiful. Look for what you haven't seen before. Engage with nature; you are literally taking the time to smell the roses.

What might seem difficult at first will gain momentum. You'll notice a flower, petals, and maybe even thorns. Thorns—how exciting! How the heck did nature come up with that? And look at the subtleties within the petals, the different pinks, reds, or yellows.

And now you might find a bug or a worm—bugs, especially big ones like cicadas or grasshoppers—are incredible machines, impressive instruments. Perhaps you'll be lucky enough to find a dead one so you can get close and study it. They are beautiful works of art.

This is a snapshot of what you do in the Finding Awe exercise. You'll find what you are looking for, so look for beauty; look to find awe, whether it's a dead bug or speckles in the asphalt.

By shifting your awareness to awe, you're cultivating a positive mindset. So the next time you're driving home and find yourself stuck in traffic and there's nothing you can do about it, you'll look for what's good about this extra pocket of time and put on a great podcast or call a friend you haven't connected with in years instead of fuming about it.

All too often, a client will tell me they had a great interview with a new company, exchanged some positive emails, set up a second interview, and then—nothing. The hiring company completely "ghosted" my client (this happens with unfortunate frequency). Now of course, this is completely unprofessional behavior, and everyone deserves a courtesy call notifying them they are no longer being considered for a role, and ideally, why. When the call doesn't come, I remind my clients that the company has done them a favor by not hiring them. It's a blessing in disguise, as you wouldn't want to work for a company like that. (I can just hear the "well, you wouldn't want to marry a man who treats you like that, dear" conversation that millions of mothers have had with their heartbroken daughters over the years). It's a small solace, and the words seem to work better in conversations of employment than of the heart.

When you foster positivity, you will have a strong framework in place in your life so negative thoughts and experiences can't hijack your emotions.

SILENCING YOUR INNER CRITIC

To start moving toward your Goal, you need to send your inner critic on vacation for a little while. Good, solid criticism can be helpful as you hone your process. However, in the early phases of clarifying and pursuing your Goal, a critic is not helpful (for a more detailed explanation, read about the Disney Model in Chapter 6).

Think of the critic as if it were snow, covering everything with a cold layer. You can't have snow when it's 70 degrees outside, it's just not possible. The early phases of setting and pursuing your Goal need those nice seventy-degree days. Your Goal can't grow in the snow. In time, we can introduce the snow—just not now.

In these early phases, criticism is not useful. Positivity is that seventy-degree day we seek.

So how do you silence your inner critic? First, observe her—and don't succumb to her. This means catching yourself when you have a negative thought. Some clients have used the old associative trick of putting a rubber band around their wrist, and when they have a negative thought, they lightly flick it. Alternatively, you can "earn" something special as a reward for observing all those instances of negative thoughts. A treat could be buying those new shoes you've had your eye on, or something you wouldn't ordinarily do for yourself. Once you catch yourself having a negative thought and stop yourself twenty-five times, treat yourself to that special thing.

You may need to call on your partner, best friend, or a family member to help with this one. Ask, "Hey, if you notice me telling you a story about why I can't reach a goal, or anything else negative, just give me a look. Or say 'watermelon' (or some other safeword)."

MY BEST SELF

Our final exercise from the Greater Good Science Center is called "My Best Self." My clients have used it, customized it, and tweaked it for all kinds of situations—it's definitely a practice favorite.

Block out fifteen minutes, and start writing about your best self in the future. It could be next year, or five years, or fifty years from now. The important thing is to just keep writing about what your best life looks like. Here's what you look like. Here's who you're surrounded by. How is your health? How do you spend your weekends? Vacations? What surprises you? Do you volunteer? What crazy things have you crossed off your bucket list? What are your finances like? Visualizing the amazing life you could have is powerful and exciting. It can lead to a sense of elation.

Practice this daily, until you feel good about it. And then think about how your Goal plays into this life. Is it a critical component?

POSITIVITY, POSSIBILITY, AND OPPORTUNITY

Throughout this chapter, we've looked at how positivity creates possibility and opportunity. We've explored how white-knuckling it through tough situations isn't the best coping strategy and how, instead, negative scenarios can be reframed as positive ones (falling up). I've also shared 3 specific exercises for reflecting on what's terrific about your life, finding awe in the ordinary, and developing a long-term vision of your best self, which are essential for achieving a positive mindset and gaining momentum toward your Goal.

INSIGHTS & ACTIONS

INSIGHTS

Please identify three to five Insights from this chapter. What are you thinking about now, that you weren't thinking about before you read this chapter? How does it apply to your Goal?

1.

2.

3.

4.

5.

ACTIONS

> Complete the Three Good Things exercise five times this week. *Tip: Do this before bed for a great night's sleep!*
> Take at least one "Awe Walk" this week.
> Complete the "My Best Self" exercise.

What are three to five Actions you'd like to take toward your Goal before the next chapter?

1.

2.

3.

4.

5.

PREP SHEET

Please complete the following questions before you begin the next chapter:

MY GOAL IS:

_____

_____

WHERE AM I, ON A SCALE OF 1 TO 10, TOWARD ACHIEVING MY GOAL?

$$\longleftrightarrow \quad\quad\quad\quad\quad\quad\quad\quad\quad\quad\longrightarrow$$

1   2   3   4   5   6   7   8   9   10

WHAT HAVE I ACCOMPLISHED SINCE I BEGAN READING CHAPTER 3?

_____

_____

WHAT DIDN'T I GET DONE, BUT INTENDED TO DO?

_____

_____

WHAT OPPORTUNITIES ARE AVAILABLE TO ME RIGHT NOW?

_____

_____

BY THE END OF THE NEXT CHAPTER I WANT TO:

_____

_____

ANY INSIGHTS OR NEW AWARENESS THAT EXCITES ME?

_____

_____

FOUR

IDENTIFY AND CONNECT WITH YOUR NETWORK

IDENTIFY AND CONNECT WITH YOUR NETWORK

x ◆──────────→ ●

In the first few chapters of this book, you've laid the foundation to pursue your Goal. You have clarified and committed to your SMART Goal (or identified a new one). You've reviewed what's terrific about your life in the Whole Life Model, gained tools to reinforce your happiness, and are practicing happiness techniques.

This is the prep work for going after your Goal, like strength conditioning. Do you remember the movie *The Karate Kid*, where Mr. Miyagi had poor Daniel paint fences and wax floors? Remember when Daniel revolted? He was mad! He was sick of all the practice work and wanted to get to the kicking and the punching. Like Mr. Miyagi, I don't want you to go out there until you're ready to win. I want you to nail your first challenge, and I want you to feel so good about it that you can't wait for your next one.

My expectation is that by now, you feel amply warmed up and ready for the more challenging work that will take you to your Goal.

Are you here? Champing at the bit? Let's crank up the level of challenge and do this!

EW, NETWORKING

The word networking draws a visceral response from so many people. They cringe, wince, or shrug back into themselves. Why is it this way? Most people associate networking with inauthenticity. They think it's more about transactions and asking for favors, a "what can you do for me, what can I do for you" affair. Which can feel gross.

When you think about networking, what is your reaction? Even though you have just been through the happiness chapter, you *can* be negative here if you need to be.

ACTION STOP POINT

- × When you read "networking," what are the first ten words that come to mind? Be honest and write them all down. What do you think networking is?

- × If you were to put a very positive spin on networking, what would it be?

- × What are some positive attributes of networking?

- × Name three people you know who are terrific networkers. Why?

If your reaction to networking was even a bit negative, then do I have a treat for you! By the end of the chapter we will have redefined "networking" and, as a result, you will be buzzing with positive memories, thinking about some of your favorite experiences and favorite people.

RETHINKING NETWORKS

Networking, first and foremost, is about connecting (or reconnecting) with people you love. When I think of networking, I think about strengthening existing positive relationships. That could include writing a thank you note to your first-grade teacher or your high school drama teacher. That's networking. It's sending out holiday cards, or reaching out to a friend on their birthday. It's the 250 people who you heard from on Facebook when it was *your* birthday. Your network is all the real, unforced relationships you have—the people who love you and who you love back.

For the first thirty years of my life, my father worked for a series of Japanese companies. He was the one of the very few Caucasian men employed by these firms, and most of the U.S.-based team was Japanese.

When his boss or other Japanese colleagues would visit the U.S., it was expected that my father would invite them to our home. He bought me a kimono, and I would dress up to welcome these Japanese businessmen into our home with, "*konbanwa*" (good evening). Later, my father and these Japanese businessmen would leave the house to wine and dine around town. Dad would wake me up at one o'clock in the morning to give me a taste of sushi—it was quite a thrill for little eight-year-old me.

The Japanese men in his company built relationships for generations. This was not exclusive to my father's company, it's a well-documented part of Japanese culture. Their business relationships are relationships first, business second. They are relationships for life, bonds that endure. I take my philosophy of networking from these early, authentic experiences I observed and participated in.

ACTION STOP POINT

× List at least seventeen* people (who are not blood relatives) you reach out to (or hear from) on birthdays, special occasions, and holidays. That group of friends you went away with for your 50th birthday, or the folks who stood up for you at your wedding. (Feel free to go past seventeen if you're feeling inspired.)

YOUR NETWORK IS YOUR LIFE'S WORK

Your network is made up of the people who want the best for you. This is about who you already know, not networking to new people. Your network isn't that guy you took a math class with twenty years ago. That's just the past.

Your current network is the people right now who are actively in your life. Who have you been in contact with over the last year? If you know your barista's name and he knows yours, then your barista is in your network. Who have you been in touch with repeatedly, or had good conversations with in the last year? **Your current network is bigger than you think.**

People *are* rooting for you, either publicly or quietly—hopefully your parents and siblings, and more. People who you haven't thought about in a decade would be thrilled to hear from you. I know that if I showed up on my first-grade teacher Mrs. Birnbaum's doorstep, she would be thrilled. In middle school and in high school I would visit her, and I

---

* Why seventeen? Well, it got your attention, didn't it? Fifteen or twenty would have been more expected here. Those are ordinary round numbers; you're accustomed to seeing them, and that makes this challenge seems more like a chore. Seventeen is prime! Strange, somewhat awkward, and it makes you take notice. I want you to look at your life a little differently. Who do you know who looks at life differently? Put them on your list.

just heard (via Facebook) that someone I know runs into her every year in Florida. I know that she invested so much into me that she would smash down any obstacle if it might help me professionally. Who are your Mrs. Birnbaums?

My teachers, my colleagues, my high school friends, the people in my life who root for me, are in my network. When I wrote cookbooks, these people were the first to buy them. When the Boston Globe reviewed my first cookbook, one of the smartest kids in my high school class clipped it and mailed it to me saying how proud he was of me. I've never gone to him for specific help, yet I know he's ready to help me if I need him. These aren't people I know professionally. They're simply people who are on my side in life.

They say the most wonderful part of having a romantic partner is that they are a witness to your life with you. But my romantic partner didn't know me in elementary school, high school, college, or the first decade and a half of my professional life. I've had many witnesses to my life, and so have you! You've probably enjoyed Facebook relationships that are celebratory and positive, fun and happy. You have witnessed each other during major life events, births of children, marriages, all causes to celebrate!

Who else is in your network? That boss who helped you in your twenties. That college professor you worked on a research project with—didn't he write your referral for grad school? Your hard-ass baseball coach from high school, your Brownie troop leader! Your CCD teacher, your best friend's mom, and your mom's best friend.

Your network is the people who are witnesses to the occurrences and important events in your life, who would go to bat for you. They've observed and helped as you became you. If "you are the company you keep," they are in fact, a part of you.

ACTION STOP POINT

× Who can you remember from elementary school who was a witness to important things that happened in your life at that time?

× What about middle school? It might be difficult to think of people, so dig deep. Who did you sit with at lunch? Was there a guidance counselor, gym teacher, or band teacher?

× What about high school, who was there? A tutor? Coach? Art or music teacher?

× List *at least* seventeen *more* people who are witnesses to your life (including the above).

WHY IDENTIFYING YOUR NETWORK IS IMPORTANT

There are three reasons why it's essential to identify your network.

1. SOMEONE HAS DONE (OR HAS COME CLOSE TO DOING) WHAT YOU WANT TO DO.

Want to become pregnant? At forty-four? Using in vitro fertilization? You can do it; women have done that. Want to get a new job building submarines? Become a doctor? Look for love at fifty-five?

You can do that; people have done that. And the more people you meet, the closer you will get to knowing people who know people who've done (or come close to doing) exactly what you want to do. Those people, more often than not, will be happy to share their story and help you get where you want to go.

You don't get a job just by applying on LinkedIn, Indeed. com, and various corporate web sites. They are useful, and they are just one way in. You, however, want to attack this Goal on several sides simultaneously.

If you use the Six Degrees of Kevin Bacon philosophy, and you're looking for a new job in your field, or in your geographic area, you probably have fewer than six degrees of separation to someone in your target organization. That is a terrific way to pursue something you want—through knowing someone on the inside.

Alternatively, if you want to go out on your own—freelance or be a part of the gig economy—I bet you know people who do that too. Find your role models; they are closer than you may think.

2. PEOPLE WANT TO HELP YOU

x ⇥——————————→ •

Lou, a mechanical engineer who built planes, had a wife who was well into her second trimester with their first child when he decided he needed to make a career move. He tried to search for a new job while still at his current one. He found his demanding hours and long commute left no time to do so.

Lou's parents and in-laws are Chinese immigrants, and as Lou shared, "They think that if the company doesn't fire you, why would you ever leave? You don't leave a job out of your own choice. You don't leave a good job to pursue happiness elsewhere." Lou knew both sets of parents would flip if he left his company before finding a new job, so he felt stuck.

Lou had his wife's support to leave, because she was the one growing tired of his complaining about work. (She's actually the one who found me and sent him to me!) After two coaching sessions, he quit his job; he believed it was the only way he'd have the time to find a new one. In retrospect, it was a smart, brave thing to do, and at the time, he was concerned that his extended family would see it as irresponsible.

A week later, Lou managed to build up the courage to tell his mother-in-law, and guess what she did? She went to work with her network. She was retired, and had worked for twenty years at Lockheed Martin, one of the largest aerospace companies in the world. She made it her job to find people who would give her son-in-law an opportunity. By sharing the news with his mother-in-law, Lou was able to network his way into his dream job less than two months after he quit his former job. He had underestimated his mother-in-law! The very same person he was afraid to tell his news to was the one who helped Lou find his next job.

● ◦→——————→ ＊

Don't underestimate the power of anyone, especially those closest to you, to help you. If they care for you, they will do everything they can to support you to reach your Goal. They want you to be happy, and if it's within their power to help you find happiness, they will stop at nothing to do so.

3. JOY SHARED IS DOUBLED; PAIN SHARED IS HALVED

Did someone give this book to you as a gift? If so, they are number one on your list. If you gift this to someone else, say to them, "Hey, when you get to Chapter Four, put me down as the first name on your list. I'm rooting for you. I want to help you reach your Goal and find happiness."

The last, and most important reason to connect with and use your network is simply because it's good for you. Ponder this, from a January 2018 *New York Times* article:

> *"Research shows that bonds of friendship are critical to maintaining both physical and emotional health. Not only do strong social ties boost the immune system and increase longevity, but they also decrease the risk of contracting certain chronic illnesses and increase the ability to deal with chronic pain, according to a 2010 report in the Journal of Health and Social Behavior."*

The true value of a strong social network is not what it gives you with respect to this specific Goal. Its true value is what it gives you every day for your physical and emotional health. Maintaining those relationships is as important as eating well and exercising—possibly more!

ACTION STOP POINT

× List ten *more* people in your life's network.

× Dig a little deeper: Who was your first boss? Your first colleagues? Did anyone help you get that first job interview? Who were your college advisors?

× What were your jobs as a kid? (Yes, babysitting counts.) Who are some adults that have known you since you were young? Non-blood related Aunts or Uncles?

SMILE BACK AT YOUR PAST

Take a moment to think of a wonderful person from way back when in your life. Why are you thinking about this person ten, twenty, or forty years later? Of all the people you've encountered, why them? What is the significant impact they had on your life?

ACTION STOP POINT

×   Who is a person, currently living, who has impacted you in a positive way (and perhaps doesn't know how much of an impact they had)? Perhaps someone you haven't connected with for a while?

×   What's a strong memory you have of this person? Please share it—the more detailed, the better. When is the last time you connected with this person?

×   Who are two more people who've had a positive impact on you? What made you think of them? Why did they have a positive impact?

×   Who do you hope you've had a positive impact on? Can you list three people, not family, and how do you hope you've impacted them?

Enjoy these memories for now. Sink into them. Enjoy these dear people as if they were sitting next to you.

ACTION STOP POINT

×   Write a letter to one person on your list to let them know how much they meant to you. Let it be at least five hundred words. Remember times you've shared, something they did for you, a look in their eye, trouble you got into together, something silly that happened with a third party. Share why you remembered them and how they had an impact on your life. Take a moment to let them know how you're different today because of knowing them. Tell them how they helped you become who you are, how your interaction with them shaped you in some way. Often, just writing a letter can fill you with emotion and beautiful tears. If you can, deliver the letter in person. Aim to read it to them in person, on the phone or via Skype. Create an opportunity to reconnect and share that joy.

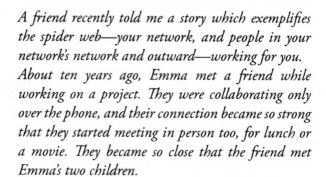

A friend recently told me a story which exemplifies the spider web—your network, and people in your network's network and outward—working for you. About ten years ago, Emma met a friend while working on a project. They were collaborating only over the phone, and their connection became so strong that they started meeting in person too, for lunch or a movie. They became so close that the friend met Emma's two children.

Then, quite suddenly, Emma's life dropped out from under her. Her son was diagnosed with leukemia and required the most intensive treatment of any cancer due to his age. Consequently, Emma lost touch with this friend.

Emma's son eventually made a miraculous, against-all-odds recovery. Emma felt guilty about losing the connection to her friend, and for years she couldn't get it out of her mind that the woman might have thought Emma just started ignoring her. Well, Emma knew this woman's birthday; she had been invited to her 50th birthday party. Even though Emma had never met her friend's husband, he had tracked Emma down to send her an invitation.

Emma did not attend the party. Three or four years later, on the day she knew was her friend's birthday, Emma wrote to her.

"When I met you, I thought you were just wonderful," Emma wrote, before letting the lady know why she had lost contact with her. "I'm very sorry that I lost touch with you. You're like sunshine. I hope you're having a really great life and a really happy birthday. Love, Emma."

That was it. Emma didn't expect anything, just like I asked you to reach out to people and not expect anything. The next thing Emma knew, her friend immediately wanted to reconnect. Emma had to tell her she didn't have a car anymore because of the financial stress of her son's treatment. The friend she said she'd come pick Emma up.

On the way to dinner, Emma confided that she was unhappy with her family's living situation and was looking for a new home. Emma's friend immediately offered up the spare mother-in-law suite in her own home.

Emma reached out to reconnect with an old friend. That was it, no agenda. And due to the authentic strength of the relationship, and a bit of serendipity, a very important life change was in store for Emma. This is the power of authentic relationships; they endure no matter how much time has passed.

REFLECTION STOP POINT

× Have you ever lost touch with someone and subsequently reconnected? What happened when you reconnected? What feeling did you have? What other events happened in your life because of this reconnection?

ACTION STOP POINT

× List at least ten people from your past who you'd like to reach out to.

× Is there someone you've fallen out of touch with who had a big impact in your life? Can you reach out to them?

× Is there someone who you adore, who's special, who you want to take a moment to acknowledge? Or is there someone you lost touch with?

YOUR NETWORK IS BIG!

As you've read this chapter, if you've been doing all the exercises, you will probably have noticed how big your list of people has grown! You may be in the triple digits by now. And that's just the tip of the iceberg. If you've been on LinkedIn or

Facebook, you know how quickly your network can grow. It's not just who you know, **it's who everyone you know knows.** We're stepping off digital networks for the purposes of this experiment and calling in the best personal computer in the world—your own brain—to recall those connections, as they are important to you. You've remembered those people and accessed positive emotions and good feelings.

These people are your network of positive connections. They are rooting for you. You, by thinking of them, are loving them, remembering them, cherishing them. Even if you don't think about them often, you have incredibly positive associations with them. That is the foundation of the network that will support you and help you make this next big move. Your Goal might be a career change. It might be rebuilding after divorce. What an important time to call upon the positive strength of your network!

CONNECT THE DOTS

Once you have your list of people in your network, connect the dots. I like to do this on a spreadsheet. You may want to do it on large piece of paper, a white board, or even stickies on a wall. Relate your people to your Goal.

›   Where do they work? What's their profession? Have they done something big in their career?
›   Do they have a marriage that you admire?
›   Do they have a big network and enjoy putting people together?
›   What about them is relevant to your Goal? Might they know someone who could help you advance your Goal?

INSIGHTS AND ACTION

INSIGHTS

What was most useful in this chapter?

Look back, and look at the headings. Look at the things you circled or highlighted. What was most useful? Recall at least three:

1. ....

2. ....

3. ....

4. ....

5. ....

ACTION

> Write (and share) a letter of thanks.
> Create a spreadsheet with your network, and connect the dots. What categories are relevant to your Goal?
> What's your positive practice for the week (from Chapter 3)? How will you implement it?

What are your three next steps toward your Goal:

1. ....

2.

3.

4.

5.

PREP SHEET

Please complete the following questions before you begin the next chapter:

MY GOAL IS:

....

....

WHERE AM I, ON A SCALE OF 1 TO 10, TOWARD ACHIEVING MY GOAL?

◆▸————————————————————————————————▶

1   2   3   4   5   6   7   8   9   10

WHAT HAVE I ACCOMPLISHED SINCE I BEGAN READING CHAPTER 4?

....

....

WHAT DIDN'T I GET DONE, BUT INTENDED TO DO?

....

....

WHAT OPPORTUNITIES ARE AVAILABLE TO ME RIGHT NOW?

....

....

BY THE END OF THE NEXT CHAPTER I WANT TO:

....

....

ANY INSIGHTS OR NEW AWARENESS THAT EXCITES ME?

....

....

FIVE

CONNECT WITH AND EXPAND YOUR NETWORK

CONNECT WITH AND EXPAND YOUR NETWORK

In the last chapter, my objective was to help you identify your existing network. In this chapter, I'd like to help you expand that network, asking the people you know to help you as you move toward your Goal. To best accomplish that, you'll need to get clear on what you need (and what you have to offer). Most importantly, I'd like to help you connect in a way that makes you feel good about asking for—and receiving—help.

REFLECTION STOP POINT

×   Have you ever introduced two people? Have you ever helped someone meet their spouse? Get a new job? Make a friend in a new town? Recount the entire story; put yourself back in that time and place. How did it benefit the individuals?

×   How did it make you feel?

× Dig deep—try to remember two or three occasions when you made an introduction for someone that was useful to them.

When you think about expanding your network, asking the people you know to make introductions for you, remember that you are inviting those people to do good and feel good.

You do an act of hesed when you make a shidduch, as my Jewish grandmother would have said.

What's that now?

Just like we drew inspiration from Japanese customs in the last chapter, in this chapter we'll continue to consider new ways of looking at situations based on other cultures' habits.

I am Jewish, and I find there are many concepts in the religion and culture that are applicable to my coaching work. Take the Hebrew word "*hesed*," for example. *Hesed* is defined as "loving-kindness, grace, and compassion." It is an action that is undertaken based on love or compassion for another.

"*Shadkhan*" is a Hebrew term for a matchmaker, and "*shidduch*" is the match. The song "Matchmaker" from *Fiddler on the Roof* is about a woman imagining what a good *shidduch* the *shadkhan* may bring her way.

The concept of a good *shidduch* expands beyond dating and marriage. A business introduction can be a *shidduch*, as can a friendship introduction for someone new in town. A *shidduch* is just another way of saying a match, whether it's friends, business partners or lovers. If you make a *shidduch*, you're a *shadkhan*.

Ultimately, asking for a *shidduch* is a good thing. It's reaching out, asking for help, giving someone an opportunity to do an act of *hesed*.

No matter what you call it—*shidduch*, networking, making a match—when you ask someone to make a connection for you, it gives them the opportunity to perform an act of *hesed*, or participate in your life in a compassionate way. By doing this, they are helping you and engaging in "*tikkun olam*"—repairing the world. You are giving your *shadkhan* an opportunity to make the world a better place.

Let me introduce one more Yiddish term: "*shep nachas*," which is the pleasure you derive from someone else's accomplishments.

Hearing that your best friend is getting married or having a baby, or that she received a major promotion at work, gives you the opportunity to *shep nachas*. It refers to the tingling joy you experience when you hear of a loved ones' good news.

When you call someone to say, "I'm engaged!" and they get all excited—they *shep nachas*. If you tell them that you are marrying the person they introduced you to—they were your *shadkhan* and they made this *shidduch*—you can imagine that their feeling of joy is uniquely exquisite.

And when you have good news to share, and you share it with those close to you, you allow those people to *shep nachas*, to be "in" the joy with you.

Get it? Got it? *Mazel tov*! (Congratulations!)

TALK ABOUT YOURSELF LIKE YOUR BEST FRIEND DOES

In order to make the best use of the introductions that will be coming your way, it's best to have a handy description of who you are, what you have to offer, and what you want.

The good news is that in the first two chapters, you dug deep with SMART Goal setting and the Whole Life Model.

You know what's important to you and what you want—what you're going for, and what your Goal is.

The Art of Self Promotion by Debby Stone is a short, useful book on—you guessed it—self-promotion. I've recommended it to clients, in part because of a simple concept that helps to re-frame the way you talk about yourself. She suggests that instead of promoting yourself, promote your best friend. Instead of writing your bio, write your best friend's bio. Often we are much better at singing the praises of our loved ones than we are at singing our own.

If that's true for you, let's use that awareness as you move forward, connecting with and expanding your network: **talk about yourself the way your best friend does.**

As you pursue your Goal, you'll need to meet new people. You will need to be able to tell them who you are, what you've done, and how you can be useful to them. And of course, there will be your "ask": What do you want from them? Do you want to learn about their career transition? Do you want an introduction to so and so? Do you want to brainstorm?

Get clear on what you're asking of them and what you have to offer. Ask for what you need. The person you are speaking with wants to help. The clearer you are with what you need, the easier it will be for them to help you. Remember, they can't read your mind and you aren't being pushy—you're simply helping them help you.

x ⟶ •

Soon after I began working with Christine, a career-changing client, her brother was getting married. She had worked as the director of a school district's arts departments for a decade, and her job was eliminated. She had tried to find more opportunities in education and hadn't had success.

Though she was looking forward to the wedding, she was not looking forward to the conversations she anticipated having with well-intentioned loved ones who would be worried about her job situation. She knew people would ask what she was doing, and she didn't know how to reply.

In our work together, she was excited about the process of career coaching. She planned to take six months to travel, to reset (she was turning forty). She was also thinking of pivoting her career out of schools and into arts administration.

Although she wasn't working, she was doing a lot and had a tale to tell. What an opportunity! She was about to be in a room with a hundred people who love her and have known her all her life. This was an opportunity for her to share her story, which was, "I hired a coach, I'm taking the next six months to travel, and I'm considering a pivot into arts administration. May I call you next month to see if you know anyone in that field?"

She marched off to that wedding with a twinkle in her eye. Instead of being embarrassed of the job she didn't have, she flipped the story to focus on what she was working on. She let everyone know she was taking advantage of the down time to do something different, and saying, "Hey, I would love your help."

● ⇢———————→ ✳

REFLECTION STOP POINT

x Have you ever been introduced? At a party, before a speaking opportunity, or via email? Typically, the person doing the introducing says something nice about you. When has this happened? Who introduced you? What was said?

x If you had to give a speech and had to choose someone to introduce you, who would it be and why?

x Who do you admire? Who is someone you know that you think highly of? If you had one minute to introduce them before receiving an award, what would you say?

ACTION STOP POINT

x Think of a person you'd like to be introduced to, someone who a friend of yours knows. Play the role of that intermediary and write a letter of introduction on your behalf. Be sure to explain what you uniquely offer, what you need, and how that person would benefit from knowing you and helping you.

x Find a best friend or a partner, and write what is so amazing about them. Have them write what is so amazing about you, with respect to your Goal: Why are you the right person to do this thing right now? Can you refine the result into a bio? An introductory email?

"DO YOU HAVE FIFTEEN MINUTES FOR A FEW QUESTIONS?"

In the last chapter, Emma wrote a letter to an old friend simply to reconnect. It was agenda free; when Emma reached out, it was for no other reason than the pure joy of reconnecting with an old friend. When you remember that old friend and think, "I wonder what they're up to," you might as well reach out. You don't know what could result from creating this new possibility.

When Emma went to meet her, she wasn't thinking of asking for any favors. She did know that one of the things she needed was a new place to stay. Emma's friend immediately saw an opportunity for Emma that Emma didn't know existed—the opportunity to live in her house.

Be prepared for synchronicity, for creation, for something new to happen that you couldn't conceive of on your own.

x ◆→————————→ •

Kelly graduated from college six years ago. After college, she worked in California, the Pacific Northwest, even Alaska. When she came to me she was living at home in New Jersey, nursing an interest in urban planning, and unsure of where to start.
I asked Kelly about people who had been helpful in her professional past, and she spoke of a woman named Mary in her college career placement department who helped her score a plum job on Catalina Island. Could she be helpful now?

That week, Kelly called Mary and asked, "Who do you know in urban planning here in New Jersey?" Mary actually didn't know anyone in the area (the university was in Florida). However, Mary mentioned that one of the professors at the university was from originally from Montclair, New Jersey, which is the next town over from where Kelly grew up!

Kelly wrote an email to this professor asking if he'd be willing to speak with her, and she received a response in minutes. "How about you give me a call now? Here's my number."

Now, to say Kelly hated calling people was an understatement; I'd seen her throw a phone across a room after writing a text asking for a favor. Kelly procrastinated networking with the best of them and cringed at "bothering" or interrupting people. This time she had no choice—the professor was asking that she call. She didn't have time to overthink it, she just picked up her phone and dialed.

They had an incredible phone call. The professor knew the town well and was able to share ideas for people to contact and places to look for part-time work. All of this from her wonderful contact in the career placement department!

Kelly was able to go from a position of not knowing anybody in urban planning to being connected with the urban planning VIPs in her backyard! It was quick and easy networking.

Now Kelly was on a roll. Since she knew what she wanted, and she knew how to talk about herself in terms of what she'd done and what she wanted to do, she found herself sharing her urban planning aspirations with strangers. The next time Kelly was with her dog in the dog run, a great spot for social interactions with strangers, she casually mentioned her interest in urban planning. And don't you know it, the man she was talking with had a son in Vermont who worked in urban planning!

This kind man gave Kelly his son's phone number, and within the week, his son jumped on the phone with Kelly and had an hour-long conversation about urban planning. He helped point her in the right direction regarding continuing education and connected her to more people and programs. Kelly knew her story, knew what she wanted to do, and knew how to ask for connections—and she was growing her network when she shared her story.

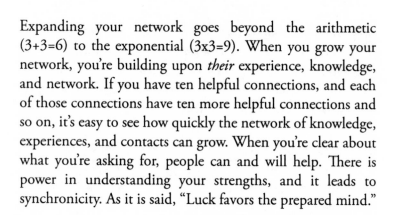

Expanding your network goes beyond the arithmetic (3+3=6) to the exponential (3x3=9). When you grow your network, you're building upon *their* experience, knowledge, and network. If you have ten helpful connections, and each of those connections have ten more helpful connections and so on, it's easy to see how quickly the network of knowledge, experiences, and contacts can grow. When you're clear about what you're asking for, people can and will help. There is power in understanding your strengths, and it leads to synchronicity. As it is said, "Luck favors the prepared mind."

THE ART OF THE INFORMATIONAL INTERVIEW

Kelly was quickly mastering the art of the informational interview—an opportunity to speak with someone who has expertise in an area you want to pursue. You are asking someone for some of their time so you can ask questions or gather information. When Kelly spoke with the professor, this was an informational interview—she wasn't interviewing for a job, she was learning about the world of urban planning from a knowledgeable source.

The urban planner in Vermont was a similar situation. There was no specific job, she was just speaking with him about his path. In an informational interview, you are connecting with someone.

The informational interview can be as simple as asking someone for twenty minutes of their time, or as formal as a sit-down interview at the place you'd like to work. You don't necessarily ask for an "informational interview," it's implied.

There are three basic phases to successfully obtaining and completing the interview:

1. The ask
2. The interview
3. Tie it up with a bow

1. THE ASK

In the stories above, you've seen a couple of successful ways to set up an informational interview—having a friend make an introduction or pursuing the contact yourself. There is one scenario that wasn't revealed; pursuing someone you don't know for an informational interview.

I'm often on the receiving end of the ask, so I can tell you what works for me. At least once a month, a coach-to-be finds me online and wants to talk to me about how I became a coach, set up my practice, etc. And I will always make myself available to someone who asks me in a professional way.

I want to see that the person has done some research about me, as well as the profession. If they are able to pull up some facts about my life (easy to find in my bio on my website), or the field in general, that's a good sign. I appreciate them asking for a specific amount of time (a twenty-minute phone call), in a specific date range. They need to let me know when they're available. Sometimes people will offer to take me out to coffee or dinner, which I sincerely appreciate. In the interest of time, I usually don't accept.

Lastly, appreciation and a desire to contribute goes a long way. When someone lets me know they appreciate me taking the time out of my schedule, or that they're young and eager to make a contribution to the field, it means something to me. I'm happy to help people with gratitude who want to contribute.

So in your ask, you want to demonstrate that you've done your homework, ask about a specific time frame (i.e. "Mondays between 7:00AM and 9:00PM EST"), and demonstrate passion/interest/gratitude.

Also—if you've reached out to someone via various methods (email, phone call, LinkedIn, and an introduction) three to five times and they aren't responding, move on. There are plenty of fish in the sea, so be sure to fish where the fish are.

2. THE INTERVIEW

The key to a good interview—any interview—is to be professional and be prepared. In terms of professionalism, there are few simple ground rules: Be early. Dress well. Initiate the call (if it's a phone call). And as soon as you start the conversation, acknowledge the kindness being extended to you—demonstrate gratitude and appreciation for the person sharing his time.

As a side note, I've always loved the saying, "Early is on time, on time is late, and late is unacceptable." The attribution ranges from business books to the Prussian army. And now that you've heard it, it's hard to get out of your mind, so you're welcome for that.

Once you've aced the above (which is truly little more than good manners), it's show time. Bring a list of questions. Seriously, have them written down or thought out. You may only ask the first one, and then you're deep into a terrific conversation. Having those questions, though, shows that you've done your research and you've been thoughtful about what you want to ask this person. They are giving you their time! For free! They could be doing anything with this time, and they've donated it to you and your future. Be careful how you spend someone else's time.

Once you start asking questions, you'll find that people love talking about themselves. Seriously. With questions like: "How did you get started in the field," "How did you choose this field and why," and "What do you like best about your field," you'll be listening. People will dig back into their past and enjoy sharing their memories with you.

And those are simply professional questions. What if you are asking a long-married couple about the success of their relationship? A woman how she was able to conceive at forty-five? A politician about how they got their first break? A female entrepreneur about how she built her business after divorce?

The conversations will be stimulating, and the questions themselves are exciting. If you enjoy preparing for your interview, your interviewee will enjoy the conversation.

Almost counterintuitively, I've found that the more successful a person is, the more likely they are to talk to you. People at the top of their game are less harried and more likely to reach back to help people who want to get started. After they've enjoyed the conversation, they may very well introduce you to more people who can be helpful.

The last two questions to ask are: "Is there anything else you think I need to know," and "Is there anyone else you think I could talk to who might enjoy a conversation like this?"

3. TIE IT UP WITH A BOW

This part, ooooh, this is the key to making this wonderful person with whom you've had a wonderful conversation part of your growing network. It's the easiest part, and 99 percent of people don't do it. This one is truly a game changer. And you're playing an A-level game, so here's the scoop:

Remember Kelly and the professor who was ready to speak with her right away? Why did he do that? What was in it for him? Well, my guess is that he was excited that this student was close to his hometown, and he was excited to talk about his past. He's also a professor, so it's fair to assume he likes teaching and growing the next generation of professionals.

Now, do you think this professor wants to hear about Kelly when she's interviewing for a job in urban planning in Montclair? With one of the people he recommended she get in touch with? You bet he does. He probably wants to know when that interview is set up—it gives him an opportunity to connect with an old colleague.

Hear me on this: The absolute key to expanding your network is reconnecting with the new people who are helping you along the way. Send a thank you note after the conversation synthesizing your takeaways—what you learned from them and why it was valuable.

You may want to send a small token of your appreciation, such as a book, a bottle of wine, or something else that was relevant to your conversation. That's memorable.

Then, follow up! If you used their suggestions or recommendations, or followed up with their contacts, let them know. Follow up six months later when you get that job. Follow up two years later when you get a promotion. Trust me, they want to know. Remember, this is the opportunity to return the favor and let them *shep nachas* with you!

There is an art to the informational interview, and once you've nailed it, you will have another person rooting for you (and your career). This is the most authentic way to expand your network.

x ◆〉————————〉 ●

Five years ago, my realtor approached me to see if I would speak with Bobby McFarland, the son of a friend. He had recently graduated from college and wanted to get into cooking (at that time, I was regularly appearing as a cooking expert on the Today Show, had published two cookbooks, and had my own cooking and travel show on Yahoo).

I told my realtor to have Bobby to reach out to me, so he wrote me a lovely email asking if he could take me out for a cup of coffee. I accepted. When he showed up to coffee, Bobby had a copy of my cookbook in his arms, which he asked me to sign. Then he told me which recipes he had tried and which he loved. I was impressed. Bobby had taken the time to buy my book, learn about what I do, and recreate my recipes. He took his time getting to know more about me before he asked for my help. He brought his A-game. Before we even took our first sip of coffee, I was already thinking about who I could introduce him to.

Bobby had just graduated college and wanted to break into cooking. He adored food personalities (especially Alton Brown) and possibly wanted to become one himself some day. More than anything, Bobby just loved cooking.

He knew he was going to pursue food as more than a hobby, and he wanted my help to think through the best way to do it. Was culinary school the best way in, or was there a better alternative? He had just graduated from college. Was more (expensive) schooling the only way in?

I reached back to the advice I had received when I was deciding whether or not to go to culinary school. A friend knew Tom Colicchio (of the Craft restaurant and "Top Chef" fame), and scored me an opportunity to observe the operations of his kitchen for a night (this is the culinary equivalent of an informational interview, except while you're standing in the kitchen, they give you lots and lots and lots of food to taste).

Tom told me that you don't need to go to school to learn how to cook; you need to learn to cook to learn how to cook. If you show up in the right kitchen, with the right attitude (and in the kitchen, a beginner attitude is far more important than knowledge), that's the way to learn.

After all, Tom Colicchio never went to culinary school, and he's doing pretty well.

So I shared Tom's advice with Bobby. I told him that the number one thing he needed to do that would differentiate him from other food personalities (if that was his end goal), was to be able to cook. It might seem like common sense, but there are plenty of food writers who can't cook. I suggested he bypass expensive culinary school and build his chops in New York City kitchens. I also recommended he continue to bring his A-game: Be in the kitchen first, leave the kitchen last, work hard, and make your commitment to the craft clear. If he could do that, he'd move up fast.

And Bobby, because he is an A-player, did just that. He went to work at some exceptional restaurants in Manhattan. Within three years, he was recruited to be the Chef de Cuisine at a new restaurant called Royale that was opening in North Carolina, and he is now the Executive Chef of their second restaurant, Lucarne. In their first year, they were honored as the best new restaurant by a local magazine.

Bobby did it. And he's just getting started.

Bobby reached out to me because I was doing what he wanted to do. I was on camera, I was writing cookbooks, and I was cooking.

So here's the takeaway: Reach out to the people who have obtained the Goal you seek. More often than not, they will make time for you. In fact, it's quite flattering to have someone want to learn from your story.

As for tying it up with a bow? One week after our conversation, Bobby hand-delivered two pounds of bacon *that he had made* to my house. It was the best bacon I have ever had. Ever. And I can't buy it—it was a homemade gift bestowed upon the lucky by one fabulously talented up-and-coming chef. My husband still talks about that bacon.

And since that time, Bobby and I have kept in touch. Last year, I featured him on my podcast, Find My Thrive. He was the most popular guest. And now instead of him asking me for my story, I'm writing about his.

Can you feel the *nachas* I'm *shepping*? Ah, the joy! The thrill of watching someone become their best self! I'm *plotzing**!

ACTION STOP POINT

× You identified three people you don't currently know and would like to meet in the last section. Write a list of ten questions, per person, that you'd like to ask them. Don't over think it, just roll. There's a reason you want to meet them.

× Who have you connected with already that you might want to reach back to and thank? Who can you reach out to and express gratitude? Think of three to five people, and write those notes. Again, don't overthink it. People enjoy hearing from you. The entire holiday card industry is built on this premise for a reason. A personalized hello is wanted, appreciated, and can often make someone's day.

YOU'VE GOT THIS

If you have a network of one thousand people, and each of those people have a network of one thousand, you're very

---

* *Plotzing* is yet another Yiddish word, in this case meaning to emotionally burst or fall over with excitement.

well connected. Think of yourself sitting on a node of a web with one thousand spokes. And each of those spokes lead to another node with one thousand spokes. Soon, you'll realize how incredibly well connected you are in a tight network. The people you want to know (and don't know yet) are often within your network.

Life is full of opportunities, and we don't all know about the same ones. The people around you know about opportunities you're not aware of. Chances are, if they know you're looking, they would love to share what they know.

Let your friends introduce you and expose you to opportunity. When the people who adore and love you connect you to others, those others are predisposed to like you because of your common denominator. Have your friends make introductions whenever possible, so everybody is primed for a positive relationship. Of course, once your friend has written that email, it's on you to follow up. You still have to be your own advocate to make things happen, even when you're accepting the help of your network.

It's your responsibility to take the hand that's extended to you.

And just like you tied up your informational interviews with a bow, it's important to circle back to your friend who made the connection for you. Remember, they are invested in you too.

Be sure to express the gratitude. That's part of happiness. Go back to Chapter 3 if you've forgotten how beneficial that is. And remember, these same people who are helping you today may come to you one day because someone they know needs your help. Let them know you'll be there for them as well. You've been helped, prepare to be helpful. You are a node on the network; someday someone will be grateful to speak with you.

INSIGHTS & ACTIONS

INSIGHTS

What was the most relevant framework in this chapter? What comes to mind without looking back? Think of at least three:

1. _____

2. _____

3. _____

Turn back the pages, and review the headings. Look at the things that you circled or highlighted. What was most useful? Recall at least three:

1. _____

2. _____

3. _____

4. _____

5. _____

ACTIONS

Identify three Actions in this chapter and complete them.

1. _____

2. _____

3.

Identify five Actions steps toward your unique Goal that you can pursue this week.

1.

2.

3.

4.

5.

PREP SHEET

Please complete the following questions before you begin the next chapter:

MY GOAL IS:

....

....

WHERE AM I, ON A SCALE OF 1 TO 10, TOWARD ACHIEVING MY GOAL?

| 1 | 2 | 3 | 4 | 5 | 6 | 7 | 8 | 9 | 10 |

WHAT HAVE I ACCOMPLISHED SINCE I BEGAN READING CHAPTER 5?

....

....

WHAT DIDN'T I GET DONE, BUT INTENDED TO DO?

....

....

WHAT OPPORTUNITIES ARE AVAILABLE TO ME RIGHT NOW?

....

....

BY THE END OF THE NEXT CHAPTER I WANT TO:

....

....

ANY INSIGHTS OR NEW AWARENESS THAT EXCITES ME?

....

....

SIX

FRAMEWORKS THAT ELEVATE THINKING AND INSPIRE MOMENTUM

FRAMEWORKS THAT ELEVATE YOUR THINKING AND INSPIRE MOMENTUM

x ✦→————————→ ●

Welcome to Chapter 6. You're more than halfway through the book at this point, which means that by now you have a clear **SMART** Goal that withstood the test of your Whole Life Model. Your foundation has been set, you have an active positivity practice, and you are feeling strengthened by the power of your growing network.

Every chapter, you're moving closer to your Goal with customized Action items that you set. There's still work to be done, and the next two chapters will help with that.

Chapters 6 and 7 are the Actions chapters, the brains and the brawn, the engine of your Personal (R)evolution. Chapter 6 is brainy and academic, with plenty of scientific studies and frameworks that will elevate your thinking. Chapter 7 will be the muscle, more tactical, providing tools to help you break through any stuck points.

If you're "in it," working hard to pursue your Goal, you may be looking at the trees and missing the forest. Chapter 6 will take you out of your thoughts, so you can be an observer of your own brain. It's a big-picture chapter, so you'll have the opportunity to step back from your day-to-day, observe yourself in action, and reframe the way you're approaching your work so that you can be (even) more efficient.

I like to think of them as the brains (Chapter 6) and the brawn (Chapter 7) of the book.

Take the time you need with Chapters 6 and 7, feel free to revisit and complete the exercises until you are knocking on the door of your Goal. Chapter 8 is the final push. Before you even begin Chapter 8, you'll need to be responding with "9" on your prep sheet when asked, on 1 to 10 scale of "How close am I to achieving my Goal?" Where are you now? How far do you have between you and a 9?

Chapters 6 and 7 will accelerate your motion. If you're lacking inspiration, keep reading. If you're having a hard time focusing, keep reading. If you're feeling stuck, *you guessed it*, keep reading. This is where you un-stick yourself.

Take a good hard look at your Goal. Is it taped to the bathroom mirror? Does it still make sense? Do you need to tweak and refine it?

In this chapter, I will cover the following concepts. You may already be familiar with some of them:

› The Pygmalion Effect
› Scarcity and Abundance Mindsets
› Heuristic and Algorithmic Workstyles
› The Prerequisites to Flow State
› Self-Compassion
› The Disney Model

THE PYGMALION EFFECT

In the 1960s, psychologist Robert Rosenthal conducted research to determine whether the notion of the self-fulfilling prophecy was true. Rosenthal's research (and subsequent book, *Pygmalion in the Classroom: Teacher Expectation and Pupils' Intellectual Development*) is one of the most well-known psychology experiments ever conducted.

Rosenthal gave intelligence tests to elementary school students in the beginning of the school year to determine the children's potential for growth, and followed up at the end of each year with a similar test to see if the predictions bore out.

However, Rosenthal did one tricky thing. After the test at the beginning of the year, he took a couple of children who were scoring in the middle of the pack and told the teachers that *these* were the children with the greatest potential. The teachers were told to treat these children the same as the rest, to not spend any extra time with them (the teachers were told they would be observed to ensure they did not).

At the end of the year, even though these children were statistically average, they were scoring with their high-achieving peers.

Voilà! The Pygmalion Effect. The teachers, likely through subconscious behavior, elicited the very results they expected to find. They created the students they expected to have.

There's a pithy quote I often see traveling around social media: "Whether you believe you can or you can't, you are right." That's shorthand for the Pygmalion Effect.

As Shawn Achor says in *The Happiness Advantage*, the Pygmalion Effect is "when our belief in another person's potential brings that potential to life."

As a coach, I'm actively engaging in the Pygmalion Effect. I believe in my clients so that they can believe in themselves and their aspirations. It's a beautiful thing to watch—ask any teacher, parent, or sports coach. When you believe in someone, they can start to see their own potential.

All humans have the ability to make a case for exactly what we want to do, describe how it's going to happen, and identify the skills we need to do it. Unfortunately, just as quickly, we can make a case as to why the world is set against us and it can't happen. My job as a coach is to help you build the case for why you can, and step away from the negative self-talk.

To establish and raise your bar, please answer the following questions. **Let's look at how far you've come and take it to the next level. You've got this.**

REFLECTION STOP POINT

× Recall a time in your life when you accomplished something difficult. (Examples include: running a marathon, winning a race, various sporting competitions, musical achievements, giving birth, completing an advanced degree—anything where hard work paid off.)

× How did you feel pursuing this goal? How did you feel when you finally achieved this accomplishment?

× How did you use that skill in the future?

ACTION STOP POINT

× Take a look at your Goal. Why are you the right person to achieve it? What are the skills you have that will help you do it? What personal strengths do you have that will take you over the finish line?

× Why is this the right time, and why are you the right person, to do this thing?

× Once you're clear on the above two points, please say it out loud, into a recorder or on a video. Keep a record of you saying these words.

× Interview a friend or loved one who believes in you. Ask them the two questions above. Record their responses.

× Refer to this video until you achieve your Goal.

SCARCITY AND ABUNDANCE MINDSETS

Experts often use the phrases "scarcity mindset" and "abundance mindset" when discussing the way people relate to money. It's rather self-explanatory: either you have a mindset that you're in danger of losing things—and thus you hoard, holding on to what you have in a desperate attempt to not lose it, or you're of the mindset that things will come as you need them, and rely on the potential of the future.

People approach their lives, and the various subsections of life (like those areas you identified in the Whole Life Model), with either a scarcity or abundance mindset. You've developed your mindset with the life you've led, influenced by your family and friends. You may have had one perspective until you went to college, and then it radically shifted (and potentially shifted back again). Your mindset can impact your perspective on friends, your home, travel, vacations, how you spend your time—everything.

I find that in working with coaching clients, those with an abundance mindset more easily pursue and achieve their Goals. In fact, a lot of my coaching involves helping my clients shift their mindset from scarcity to abundance, preparing them to welcome the possibility of their Goal being achieved. Anyone can evolve and shift their mindset if they want to.

Let me say that again, because it's important: **Anyone can evolve and shift their mindset if they want to.** It's completely within your control, just like practicing happiness can shift your feeling of enjoyment and contentment.

Take a look at these actual quotes from my clients, and identify whether they're in a mindset of scarcity or abundance:

"If I quit this job, I'll have nothing."

"The only way for me to search for the job I want is to leave this job I hate. I'm quitting this week so that I'll free up more time to find the next thing (and I'll probably find it sooner)."

"I will never find the right guy for me. And I'm definitely not dating a firefighter."

"I have to live at home because I can more easily pay off school debt if I don't take on rent."

"I can't leave New Jersey. Everything is here. It's my life."

*"I am **not** commuting to New York. I know there's more opportunity there, but I just won't do it. Never have, never will."*

When I write these quotes, they look obvious to me (and probably to you). And when I reflect these comments back to my clients, they can also step to the side and observe their perspective. When they are saying the words, the bias just spills out—and they are not aware of how biased they are within their own perspective of abundance or scarcity.

REFLECTION STOP POINT

× On a scale of (1) scarcity to (10) abundance, where are you with respect to believing you will achieve your Goal? Why? And most importantly, what would shift your thinking to a 10?

Tyson, a recent college grad, came to talk to me about his next steps. He had tried a corporate job in Manhattan, working in a cube, and it made his skin crawl. He left and was living "down the shore" with his mother near Asbury Park, waiting tables during the Shore's slowest season. He needed to make at least $300 a month for his college loans. He felt tremendous pressure to get a "real" job.

He was also a musician, specifically a drummer. He had recently tweeted at his favorite band with a cover of one of their songs. The drummer tweeted back that he loved it. The band was based in Los Angeles, which was where Tyson's brother lived. He wanted to move there, but...how could he make the money he needed to pay off his college loans?

It was pretty clear that Tyson would be best served by following his passion to LA. Chances were he could make better money as a server in LA than he could at the Shore in winter. And he had a couch he could crash on for a couple months until he figured it out.

But...but...but...drumming wasn't a "real job." And how would he afford his own place? And how would he find a restaurant to work in?

These were all questions of a scarcity mindset. Tyson was only twenty-three. Could he give this a couple months just to see if he could make it happen?

Two months after our session, I received an email from Tyson. He had moved to LA. He was able to shift his mindset to seeing the abundant opportunity there. He gave himself permission to pursue his passion for music—even if it was just for a few months.

He shifted his mindset and changed this chapter of his life, perhaps rewriting the book in the process.

ACTION STOP POINT

× Let's review the sections of the Whole Life Model. For each, how would you identify your mindset? Are you coming at the topic from a perspective of "I have what I need and am certain that I'll have what I need in the future," or "I am not sure how I'll get what I need in this area of my life." Please pick one or the other; no midpoints. Here are the categories:
  × Health
  × Spirituality
  × Friends
  × Family
  × Love & Partnership
  × Personal Development
  × Fun & Creativity
  × Physical Environment
  × Finances
  × Career

× For the scarcity mindset areas, what would you need
to gain a feeling of abundance? What would shift your
thinking? Even if nothing changes, what could shift
your *thinking* in this area? Do you know anyone who
has less than you, and just has a mindset of abundance
in this area? Why do you think they might feel this
way?

HEURISTIC AND ALGORITHMIC WORKSTYLES

Author Daniel Pink, whom I mentioned in the personal
development section of Chapter 2, has a series of outstanding
books that explain people's relationship to work. (Note: If
your goal is not work related, you may want to skip this
section. Or keep reading for the pure joy of learning).

Drive: The Surprising Truth About What Motivates Us
breaks down all types of work into two categories: algorithmic
or heuristic. Algorithmic work follows a basic formula, or
algorithm. Algorithmic jobs include bank tellers, cashiers,
and certain types of accountants. This category could be (or
already has been) outsourced to computers or robots (ATMs,
automatic cashiers). Fundamentally, these jobs lack creativity;
the worker needs to complete basic tasks to achieve the same
result. It's easy to see how these jobs can be outsourced. If you
can find another source to complete the algorithm, the job
can be completed without a human.

This is not new; just think of all the machines that
do what humans used to do, like sewing clothes or filling
cans. Now, much of this is the work of machines—basic
algorithmic work.

So here's the good news: 70 percent of U.S. job growth is
in the second category, that of heuristic work, so let's get to
know that category a little better.

Heuristic work requires creativity to come up with a novel idea or solution. It is the type of work most people who come to my office want to do. Even the accountants I know are looking to add creativity to their work—for both job preservation and career satisfaction. Most people enjoy work that requires creativity outside the basic algorithm. Heuristic workers write novels, compose songs, and create ad campaigns. They build restaurants, make movies, and teach the innovative minds of the future.

REFLECTION STOP POINT

× Is your work heuristic or algorithmic? If you're looking to make a change, which category fits your ideal career?

Daniel Pink has identified the four criteria that make heuristic workers happy:
› Baseline compensation
› The opportunity for autonomy
› Mastery
› Meaningful work

Heuristic workers want to meet their financial needs. They are not necessarily looking to make a killing, they just need to make enough to pay their bills, go on vacation, and flex their creative muscles. They want their basics taken care of. **They are not motivated by money; they are motivated by the work itself.**

However, if their basic financial needs aren't met, and they are nervous, anxious, or stressed as a result, they lose their ability to work confidently (they are distracted). Heuristic workers need to have their financial needs met so they can get back to the business of doing what they love to do.

Once those needs are met, they need an autonomous workplace. They can't be told how to do what they do; they need to be trusted to do the job to the best of their ability.

Let's take an example from the domestic arena: a simple task like loading a dishwasher. Now, this looks like it might be an algorithmic task. The fact is, loading a dishwasher involves a great deal of creativity. I've seen too many clients tell their partners, "That's not the way you load a dishwasher." That continues on to, "That's not the way to change a diaper," or "That's not how you bathe the children."

Unless you want your heuristic worker to quit (and on the home front, that means that you just bought yourself a whole lot of additional chores), just stop. Let that person find their way. Micromanagement is the ultimate pain for heuristic workers, who thrive when they have autonomy.

How many workers leave their jobs and decide to work freelance or start their own companies just so they can be in charge of how they work and when? Let's be honest—it's hard to run your own company! And yet, so many people are willing to take on that challenge for the sake of their own autonomy.

Heuristic workers also need the opportunity to gain mastery in their field. They need professional challenges that are significant enough that they are motivated, and attainable enough that *with just a bit more effort* they can be reached. Heuristic workers need constant challenge and the opportunity to grow in that thing they love to do. This is what Pink refers to as the "opportunity for mastery."

Smart companies with savvy HR departments (these are usually rebranded as "Learning and Development" teams) help their employees build a development and growth plan, so the employees are supported in their quest for mastery. Licensed health professionals have this built in to their profession—they need to take continuing education classes so they can keep their license. This forces the practitioners to learn, grow, and continue increasing their levels of mastery (and practice their profession responsibly).

The old saying, "If you're not growing, you're dying," is morbid, yes, and for the heuristic worker it's completely true.

Finally, heuristic workers need an opportunity to connect with a larger purpose, to engage in meaningful work. Meaningful work is work that impacts the people around you, the world as a whole. Meaningful work means that you're connected with something larger than yourself.

The quote, "There are no small parts, only small actors," brings to light the notion of meaning. Every part in a play is important, every actor lends something to moving the story along. If you can only be happy when you play the lead, then perhaps this isn't the right work for you.

A heuristic worker doesn't need to be the top tennis player; her skills may be better suited to ball girl or coach. And she recognizes that the creative skill she brings to her job is important.

For a great example of this, Google "Airport employee dancing on the tarmac." You'll see a man whose job it is to guide airplanes out to the runway, and he's chosen to take it up a notch by also performing for the passengers because...well, I'm not exactly sure why. What I do know is that he's got a captive audience, and he's choosing to have fun with his job.

He's bringing a great attitude to his work, increasing the creativity of the job, going way beyond the job description, and having a more meaningful impact. He needs to move the plane safely, and he's increasing the challenge of his work by entertaining the passengers and pilots as he completes his job. He's giving himself the opportunity to redefine what his work is (autonomy), increasing his level of mastery (dancing while guiding the plane), and connecting with a much larger audience (he's not just working to communicate with the pilot, his audience is the entire plane—and now, the Internet, thanks to YouTube).

Does he seem happy in his work? I think so. Just have a look at him on YouTube to judge for yourself.

REFLECTION STOP POINT

× Do the fundamental requirements for satisfying heuristic work make sense to you? Can you name them and describe them? Look at the job you have: are these qualities reflected in your job? If not, why not? Can you possibly shift them? How?

ACTION STOP POINT

× If any heuristic job satisfaction criteria are not present in your job, and you've identified how you can change them, write down three things you need to do to make that change happen. Who can you speak with? What can you ask for?

THE PREREQUISITES TO FLOW STATE

The concept of flow state has become popularized since it was conceived by psychologist Mihaly Csikszentmihalyi. He has spent a lifetime studying the characteristics that enable people to be "in the zone," performing at their best. His book, *Flow: The Psychology of Optimal Experience*, was first published in 1990, and his theories are still actively in use today. You've likely heard of the concept of flow, or being "in the zone."

Csikszentmihalyi was a child during the Holocaust; at the age of ten he was on the last train leaving Hungary. As the train pulled away, he could see bombs, chaos, and terror behind him. That seminal experience set him on a quest to understand how people could get so far off track and, more importantly, how they could regain their best selves.

Eventually he made it to the United States, where he studied philosophy, decision making, leadership, happiness, and joy; he wanted to answer why people behave the way they do. He studied thought, how people felt when they were at peak, and how they could put themselves into that state.

My hope is that you're in the flow state now. If you're not, let's get you there. Csikszentmihalyi's three prerequisites to entering the flow state are:

› Clarity of goals and immediate feedback
› A high level of concentration
› Balance between existing skills and the challenge

Let's dive in to each one.

ONE: CLARITY OF GOALS AND IMMEDIATE FEEDBACK

In the first two chapters, you clarified your Goal. At the end of each chapter, the first question on your prep sheet invites you to revisit your Goal. You know what you're aiming for, and are moving toward it on a regular basis. That clarity will help you get into the flow state.

On a regular basis, you establish tactics (Actions) that move you toward your Goal. When I work with clients in my office, I recommend that they have their coaching session early in the day, if possible, because in our session they often have a series of *a-ha* moments and get clear on their strategy and the Actions they need to take. They leave my office like a slingshot and can't wait to get out into the world and get to work. Strategic clarity leads to flow.

Immediate feedback is another requirement to enter flow state, and part of the reason you write those prep sheets on a regular basis. If you're craving more feedback, I encourage you to set up a more formalized accountability relationship with someone close to you. You can share an update on a regular basis—a Personal (R)evolution check in. Let them know what's going well each week, and hear yourself say it out loud. Get your own feedback and theirs.

Let's borrow an example from sports. When a soccer coach watches her players, she'll yell to them from the sidelines, "Thatta girl, you nailed it! Now move to the goal!" and the player moves a little closer.

The immediate, real-time feedback lets a player know what's working and what they need to modify. I hope that while pursuing the exercises in Chapter 5 you received real-time feedback. You may have been nervous about expanding your network until you started receiving responses to your emails and realized that people do want to help! That feedback helps you get into the flow state ("Wow! I must be doing something right!").

Share your wins with your network and your struggles with a trusted advisor. They will help you move forward. If you're stuck on an email to send, talk it through with them today. You don't want that email sitting in your outbox for a week.

TWO: FOCUS

Focus is my word; Csikszentmihalyi describes this concept as "a high level of concentration on a limited field."

When I coach in person, all phones are off, all distracting media is shut down. My client is with me, together in our session, protected from requests for our attention from the outside world. For some clients, it's the only hour of their week they have that level of focus. Personally, I love this level of focus. After all, I see four clients per day on average, and it gives me the opportunity to zone in and focus on that person. It can be a relief to be that present. It puts me in the zone, in flow state, and it feels *good!*

Let's look at some other situations where a person is obligated to have "a high level of concentration on a limited field." On a busy night, a restaurant chef has to completely focus on preparing food and moving it out of the kitchen. Narrow focus, limited field. There's no way that chef is going to have a second to check his phone or have a conversation with his wife.

An editor working on a book needs to log out of email, refuse updates from Facebook, and put herself in a place where she can focus. A computer programmer who is trying to learn a new coding language needs to give his full concentration to that language in order to absorb it.

When you're pursuing your Goal, give yourself the chunk of time that's needed to effectively do it. For clients pursuing career-related Goals, it's much more effective to head over to Indeed or LinkedIn and give yourself an hour or two to go deep, than it is to give yourself fifteen minutes to check in. Equip yourself with big chunks of time so you can get to a high level of concentration when you're working on your Goal.

In true flow state, you can actually lose yourself in the activity and lose track of time. If you give yourself ninety minutes to dive deep in Indeed and find yourself wanting to keep going, do it! You're in the flow.

If you can only take fifteen minutes to research new contacts that can help you with your Goal, you're never going to enter flow state; it's just not enough time. Ideally, give yourself a two-hour focused block. That is more likely to put you in the flow. The time you take will be more enjoyable and more effective.

THREE: BALANCE BETWEEN YOUR EXISTING SKILLS AND THE CHALLENGE

Remember Daniel Pink's concept of mastery? That's a derivative of this concept. To illustrate the point, let's look at skiing. If you're a strong blue (beginner) skier, at some point you feel confident enough to approach a green (intermediate) run. That's a flow-appropriate level of balance (or tension) between what you can do with ease, and what you haven't done (yet).

However, if you take a blue skier to a black diamond (expert) slope, the skier will freeze with anxiety, apprehension, and fear. The balance between her existing blue skills and the black skills are too far apart; she will not approach flow state for the challenge because she'll be focused on her fear, as this is not a realistic challenge for her.

Crossword puzzle people know this drill; Sunday is the hardest puzzle of the week, and Monday is the place to start. In any martial arts practice, as you increase your skills you obtain new belts to recognize (and publicly acknowledge) your new level of skill. If the belts simply moved from white (beginner) to black (expert), without the rainbow of acknowledged achievement along the way, it would be far less motivating. The multiple levels help martial artists stay in the flow state as they pursue their goal over the many years it takes to become a master.

Csikszentmihalyi pointed out that to be in the flow state, a person needs a challenge that is just a little bit out of reach and the skills to meet that challenge.

REFLECTION STOP POINT

× Are you having trouble getting into flow state? If so, here's a flow prerequisite checklist for you.

1. Do you have clarity on your actions on a regular basis?

2. Do you have immediate feedback, positive or negative? If you don't have a coach, do you have a friend to give you that feedback? Are you sharing your wins with people on a regular basis?

3. Are you giving yourself the opportunity to single-mindedly focus on the work that is needed to achieve your Goal on a regular basis?

4. Are you striking the right balance between your existing skills and the challenge (your opportunity for mastery)?

ACTION STOP POINT

× If you've identified an opportunity to improve your approach to pursuing your Goal based on the questions above, take a moment to redirect yourself. Do you want to commit to a larger chunk of focused time? When can you schedule that this week? Are you spending enough time getting feedback on what's working and what's not? Articulate a plan (either write it down or record it on video or audio) and see it through.

SELF-COMPASSION

Dr. Kristin Neff is an associate professor in the department of Educational Psychology at the University of Texas in Austin. She is one of the world's leading authorities on self-compassion. Most people understand the importance of being kind and compassionate to others. When it comes to ourselves, however, we often use different strategies. Neff studies what happens when people are kind to themselves, treating themselves the way they treat their best friends.

Imagine that your friend has been working toward a big Goal and is mad at themselves on a week-to-week basis because there is one thing on their to-do list that never gets done. Of course, they are getting many other things done—and their focus is on that one thing that isn't happening.

How would you handle this? Most people would help their friend focus on the six things they're doing well. They'd take time to help the friend acknowledge what they have achieved, redirecting their friend to the success.

REFLECTION STOP POINT

× Have you been tough on yourself during this process? What kind of self-talk have you been engaging in?

× If it was a friend in this position instead of you, what would you say to that person?

ACTION STOP POINT

In Chapter 3, I reviewed practices for happiness, and acknowledging and quieting your inner critic was part of that practice. Self-compassion raises that practice to the next level.

× Let's reframe your inner critic (who loves nothing more to engage in negative self-talk) as a best friend. Could you wave a magic wand and turn the Wicked Witch into a Good Witch? Seriously, let's name that Wicked Witch (pick a name), and name your Good Witch.

When the Wicked one shows up, just wave your wand and replace her.

× What is something the Wicked Witch loves to talk about? Can you share her three favorite refrains?

× How would the Good Witch respond to these comments?

Increasing your self-compassion will take you to your Goal more efficiently and make the process more pleasant. If your Goal is to work out five days a week, and that level of fitness will contribute to your happiness, self-compassion is the skill of not beating yourself up over a week when you missed a workout or two. Self-compassion is what will keep you from defeating yourself by letting your inner critic wear you down or convince you to give up.

Self-compassion lets you stick to your process by protecting you from moments of self-sabotage.

Furthering one of the points in Chapter 3, the Happiness Chapter, many of us have been trained to think that achieving our goals is a matter of doggedly pushing forward; and some may call on an inner critic to push themselves. Unfortunately, that negative self-talk takes a lot of energy. You're generating the negativity and absorbing it or trying to ignore it. That whole process is distracting and can be draining, especially if you have a vociferous inner critic.

DON'T "SHOULD" ON YOURSELF

Whenever I hear the word "should" spoken by my client, my ears perk up. "Should" is a big red flag for me. In fact, when I hear that word I'll say, "Whoa, whose voice is that? You 'should'? According to whom?"

I don't let anyone "should" on my clients, and I certainly don't let my clients "should" on themselves. Their inner critic attended the school of thought that you need to push people, be hard on them. To help them achieve, they "should" do this or that. I don't subscribe to the "should" school of motivation. I believe people can achieve great things when they're calm and centered.

Self-compassion goes beyond avoiding negative self-talk. It also means treating yourself well. Take my husband for example: when he makes a sandwich, he goes all out. He toasts the bread, he gets out a tomato and lettuce, good mustard, maybe some hot peppers, too—he makes a beautiful sandwich. It takes him fifteen minutes.

Why does my husband take the time to make a good sandwich? He thinks it's worth it. *He knows he's worth it.* He treats himself well, just like he would a good friend.

On the other hand, let's look at self-denial. When my children have birthday parties, there's this moment after the children have had their cake (and they all happily gobble it up), that I'll make rounds giving cake to the adults.

Can you guess what they say? "Oh, I shouldn't. Just a bite. Just a sliver." Or, in the worst cases—and let me clearly state that I am guilty as charged on this one—the person will say, "I'll just take a bite from my kid's plate."

What? You refuse yourself something you want, and end up stealing it from someone else! So in addition to neglecting yourself, you're taking a cherished bite of cake from someone who was looking forward to it.

Self-denial has a negative impact on the people around us. They have to give up that bite of cake or that lick of their ice cream cone because you didn't want to buy a whole one for yourself. Did they agree to that deal? This illustration demonstrates the way people around you can be called upon to compensate for your martyrdom; whether it's a family that doesn't get to see you because you work long hours, a relative or friend who has to worry about your health problems because you won't see a doctor or take your medication, or a child who learns not to ask for help because you're tense and stressed from overextending yourself.

Yes, that last paragraph was a bit negative, and I hope you get my point. The idea here is to use your skill of self-compassion to acknowledge what you need and give it to yourself; because that's a good way to treat yourself, and because self-neglect can have repercussions for everyone else in your life.

The opposite of negative self-talk, "should-ing" on yourself, and denial, is to engage in an active practice of acknowledgement. As you may have noticed, in every end-of-chapter prep sheet is the question "What have I accomplished?" This is your opportunity to treat yourself like you treat your best friend—to make a list of what you've done, and put the focus there. By acknowledging the progress you've made, chapter by chapter, however big or small, you give yourself a treat. As you evaluate how far you've come, if there are things you didn't get to do, you can also acknowledge them in a healthy way. You didn't accomplish something you wanted to? Well, there must be a reason. Is it no longer important to you? Has your Goal shifted a bit? Do you need to break that down into smaller steps (more on this in the next chapter) before you go after it? Acknowledging your achievements and clarifying why the other items didn't get done will help you stay flexible and make this process fun.

REFLECTION STOP POINT

× Who do you know who treats him or herself well? Can you give some examples?

× Who do you know who doesn't take that piece of cake? How does that impact the people around them?

ACTION STOP POINT

× Let's acknowledge you! Stop and give me ten things you've done since you started this book. I'll help you out—you made it to this page! You're cooking, and you're almost there!

THE DISNEY MODEL

Walt Disney is a globally recognized leader in both creativity and productivity. As a result, researchers studied Disney to see how he did what he did. How did he have these crazy ideas, and how did he take them from concept through implementation? As a result of this research, we now have the Disney model.

Researchers determined that Walt Disney had three distinctly different modes when he engaged in the creative process. They named these modes the Creative, the Planner, and the Critic. His coworkers could identify which mode he was in because Disney would physically appear differently. He would dress differently, act differently, he became a different version of himself. He personally embodied these three different modes of being; each of these work styles were within him.

THE CREATIVE

Creative mode was where Disney would conceive ideas. This would be a protected space for creative thought, a place where he could brainstorm in the "no idea is a bad idea" space. Everything is game—the bigger and bolder and more original, the better.

When I coach, I find that clients sometimes have a tough time staying in creative mode. It's easy to timidly mention something you want to do, and then just cover it over with all the reasons it can't be done.

The creative phase is key, so when I hear my clients say phrases like "Well, what I *really* want to do," or "You know, I've *always* wanted to do," or "The thing I *wish* I could do," my ears perk up. They're about to share something from the Creative.

And too often, this is followed by a long and much more confident voice of why they can't. The Creative is small and fresh, like a new baby, and I do everything I can to protect the beautiful idea that's being shared, often for the first time, in my office.

So I push my client back into creative mode and let them spend time fleshing out the idea.

You know how people have great ideas in the shower or during a hike? Creative mode loves fresh air and nature. The creative mode loves inspiration. When you're feeling healthy and good, that's a great time to be inspired or to give voice to something you've been thinking about for a while.

In creative mode, I picture Walt Disney walking around his office like Jiminy Cricket, with a jaunty hat and coat, singing "When You Wish Upon A Star" to those who need a little time in the creative space for their vision to come alive.

THE PLANNER

Planner mode is where the rubber meets the road, where that exciting idea starts to take shape. It's where the creative idea has become strong enough and important enough to you that you can begin to think about how you can make it reality.

When you're in the planner mode, you take your inspired idea, like, let's say, putting a man on the moon, and say, "Well, first we'd need to make a rocket. Who has a rocket? How could we get a rocket?"

The Planner is a servant of the idea, doing everything he can to make that idea a reality. "So this man, the one who's going to the moon, let's think about what he'd need. He'd need to be healthy and fit. He'd also need to be able to manage in zero gravity, so I suppose we could create a zero-gravity simulation and get him prepared. What would he eat? Hmm. Freeze-dried food?"

The Planner never questions the idea; his job is to make it happen.

Although this is the Disney Model, Cirque de Soleil always comes to mind for me when I think about this phase. Have you ever seen one of their shows? People are just flipping all over the place in these incredible costumes.

My first reaction is always, "Who was capable of conceiving of this? This is insane." And then, "Even if you have this crazy idea, how did they make it come true?" That's the job of the Planner. Never question the premise, just make it so.

The Creative can talk to the Planner, because the Planner understands the Creative and their response is, "Great idea, chief. I'll get right on this." The Creative and the Planner are buddies.

While you pursue your Goal, you, just like Disney, inhabit each persona separately. Each state is needed for the creative idea to come to fruition. And for each persona to do their job to the best of their ability, they need certain things. The Creative needs private space to conceive the idea, the Planner needs to have complete faith that the idea is possible. And the Critic, well...

THE CRITIC

The Critic's job is to poke holes in the plan. Her goal is to find any weak spot, any hole, so those weaknesses can be addressed before the plan is implemented. The Critic and the Planner have a solid relationship, because the Critic is working in the service of the plan. With fresh eyes, she stress-tests the plan before it is implemented. She finds the areas that need to be bolstered before the plan can be put into effect.

You already have Critics in your life: your lawyer, the doctor who tells you that you need to lose forty pounds or else you're at risk for a heart attack. These critics aren't negative; they're trying to point out areas for improvement so you can be your best. They're an important part of your team, and they ask, "Have you thought about this? For this to work, you need to do this."

The Critic and the Planner work together to hone the plan, to make it airtight so you can implement it. They have a terrific relationship, because they want to make the best plan possible. The Planner works in the service of the idea, and the Critic works in the service of the plan. Everyone is working to make the idea come to life.

The key to making this whole system work is that the Critic can never interact with the Creative. The Critic may never, ever be in the same place or the same conversation as the Creative, because the Critic will kill the Creative. The Creative is full of life and energy, and wild, imaginative brilliance. She is also fragile, and she will wilt in the presence of the Critic.

The Critic means no harm; her job is to point out the problems—at the right place, and at the right time. If she starts pointing out the problems in the idea, as opposed to the plan, the Creative wilts and dies. And good luck getting her to come out and play again.

You can't conceive of fresh ideas if your Critic is present. You can't conjure up Cirque du Soleil while your lawyer is pointing out all the things that can go wrong. The Critic is the ultimate idea killer. **So never let the Critic in the room with the idea**; just put her in the room with the plan. *That's important.*

A lot of the work I do with my coaching clients involves making room for the Creative and drawing out the Planner. For the first few sessions, the Critic is not welcome in the room. Period. When Critic shows up, she is often a large, bloated presence—especially when she comes too early. My job is to show her the door. "I'm sorry, you're not invited in just yet. We're going to need a little more time before we've got something for you."

I'm very gentle and welcoming when the Creative shows up. Have you ever tried to connect with a wild animal? You move slowly, carefully, gently. That's what it's like to make the Creative feel safe (picture Jane Goodall in her early days with the gorillas).

Once the Creative is comfortable (and make no mistake, I've got the fly swatter out all the time when the Critic pops in—she is tenacious!), you are able to give space to the idea.

This is when I start to see the most beautiful smiles on my clients' faces. They reconnect with their hopeful selves, seeing possibility. There's no high quite as powerful as a Creative high.

After they're feeling strong in the idea, they can start planning. Again, the Critic will show up and I'll have to remind my client that it's just not time yet for the Critic. I promise, we will get there; we're just not there yet.

Unfortunately, the people in your life who love you the most and want to protect you, to keep you safe and comfortable, often show up as the Critic. It's probably best not to share the idea with them until it's a more well-conceived plan.

Part of the reason some of my clients seek out coaching is to restore balance when there's an overactive Critic and a Creative who is beaten down. I help clients quiet the Critic as they pursue something difficult. I often find myself protecting their sweet, newborn Creative idea from the Critic because if the client isn't practicing self-compassion, that Critic will kill the Creative.

Let's say you have a fruit tree that isn't bearing fruit because it has too many branches. The Critic voice will say, "If you want fruit, we're going to have to trim these branches." That's still a "yes" to fruit. The Critic's way of saying "yes" is to say, "but there's an obstacle to the 'yes' that you need to be aware of." This is healthy.

It is when your modes get out of balance, with a very active Critic (either internally, or externally in the form of another person) and an inactive Creative, that I give your Creative more space and I poke the Planner, who may have been on vacation while the Critic has been bossing the Creative around.

Culturally, there is often a prejudice against our creative voice. It's strongest in children, and it's something that people are trained to "grow out of." So in most people, the Creative is soft-spoken. It's a hopeful vision that you keep to yourself because you're afraid others will think it's silly.

Up to this point in the book, your Planner has been active. You were in planning mode every time you wrote your Action steps and when you recorded your Insights. *Having* the Insights is the work of the Creative. Capturing those Insights is the work of the Planner. *Translating* those Insights into Actions is the work of the Planner. You don't need to explicitly invite the Critic, as most people can't get their Critics to stop showing up anyway.

The Critic is your inner editor. Your dental hygienist. Your manicurist. Editing, teeth scraping, and cuticle cutting is not meant to kill or destroy you, it's meant to enhance you. The Critic doesn't want to hurt you, she wants to protect you. She will help you achieve your goal if you use her in the right way.

REFLECTION STOP POINT

× Take a moment to consider your Creative, Planner, and Critic.

× Have you let the Creative have enough time to do her thing?

× Are they collaborating well? How could you enhance their balance?

× How does this framework relate to your goal?

INSIGHTS & ACTION

INSIGHTS

What was the most relevant framework in this chapter? What comes to mind without looking back? Think of at least three:

1.

2.

3.

Turn back the pages, and review the headings. Look at the things that you circled or highlighted. What was most useful?

Recall at least three:

1.

2.

3.

ACTIONS

Identify three Actions in this chapter and complete them.

1.

2.

3.

Pursue three Action steps toward your Goal.

1.

2.

3.

PREP SHEET

Please complete the following questions before you begin the next chapter:

MY GOAL IS:

....

WHERE AM I, ON A SCALE OF 1 TO 10, TOWARD ACHIEVING MY GOAL?

1   2   3   4   5   6   7   8   9   10

WHAT HAVE I ACCOMPLISHED SINCE I BEGAN READING CHAPTER 6?

....

....

WHAT DIDN'T I GET DONE, BUT INTENDED TO DO?

....

....

WHAT OPPORTUNITIES ARE AVAILABLE TO ME RIGHT NOW?

....

....

BY THE END OF THE NEXT CHAPTER I WANT TO:

....

....

ANY INSIGHTS OR NEW AWARENESS THAT EXCITES ME?

....

....

SEVEN

DOUBT CRUSHER: TACTICAL TOOLS TO HELP YOU BREAKTHROUGH AND TAKE ACTION

DOUBT CRUSHER: TACTICAL TOOLS TO HELP YOU BREAK THROUGH AND TAKE ACTION

You have arrived! Welcome to Chapter 7, the brawny tools and tactics chapter. Chapter 6 provided you with academic frameworks to give you school smarts. This chapter is all about the street smarts. Tools you can use—right now—so you can more efficiently navigate to your Goal!

This is the penultimate coaching chapter. Your next chapter, "Closing the Deal," will take you the final mile toward Goal achievement. As I mentioned in the last chapter, before you begin the next chapter, you will be at a 9 on your 1 to 10 scale of "Where am I, on a scale of 1 to 10, toward achieving my Goal?"

So this is it! The frameworks from the last chapter and the tools in this chapter will help you take those final steps. This chapter is filled with the short cuts that well-traveled journeymen rely on, so hop into the back of my cab, I'm going to show you a route you've never seen before. Let's do this—you've got a Goal to achieve!

In this chapter, I'll review the following tactical tools:

› Unleash Your Inner Superhero
› Identify Your Stakeholders
› Let Your Role Models Pull You Up
› Milestones & Inch Pebbles
› Question Burst™
› Eustress
› Meditation

UNLEASH YOUR INNER SUPERHERO

A recent study by psychologists Rachel E. White and Emily O. Prager demonstrated the power of superhero dress up when it comes to important life skills like perseverance and persistence.

They found that children who were dressed in a Batman costume were able to spend more time working on a tedious task than others in a control group who weren't in costume.

When these four- and six-year-olds associated themselves with a hero, they behaved more heroically.

If you've ever dressed up—as a child or an adult—you know how intoxicating the experience can be. You have permission to behave how another person would. And if the proliferation of "sexy" costumes is any indication, playing dress up is a way to give yourself permission to be and do something you might not let yourself try otherwise.

REFLECTION STOP POINT

× When is the last time you dressed in a costume? How did it make you feel? What was the impact of wearing that costume? Did you act differently? How?

Amy Cuddy, Harvard professor, social psychologist, and author of *Presence: Bringing Your Boldest Self to your Biggest*

Challenges, is responsible for the distribution of the "power pose" meme. Her 2012 **TED** Talk is one of the most powerful of all time.

Based on her research, she determined that holding a power pose (think Wonder Woman or Superman, arms akimbo, legs apart, chest out) increases testosterone and reduces cortisol. In fact, after holding this pose for a short period of time (just two minutes), study participants felt more calm and confident.

By holding a power pose, one is better prepared to engage in a high-stakes situation and confidently go after success.

Since then, other academics have attempted to replicate her research and had mixed reviews. The concept has caught fire in the pop psychology world, however, and I recommend you give it a whirl.

Before that important meeting, phone call, or even just to psych yourself up for the day, try standing in a super hero power pose. I, for one, believe that even if your testosterone doesn't spike, the placebo effect is worthwhile. Taking a couple minutes breathing and standing confidently has a positive impact.

And if that doesn't work, grab a cape and a mask. Dress up is a powerful empowerment tool.

x ⟶ •

Saily Avelenda (her real name) made a significant life change after tapping into her own inner superhero. When she came to see me in the fall of 2016, she was a successful corporate attorney with a gnawing feeling that she wanted to do more.

After Donald Trump was elected, Saily was devastated. She felt like she had not done enough to help Hillary Clinton win. She was a first-generation Cuban-American, and I remember when she locked eyes with me and said, "My parents didn't come to this country for me to have opportunity so that I could become a corporate attorney. I need to do something bigger, something more. I need to make a contribution."

She became involved with several local activist groups. Their goal was to start a productive conversation with their Republican congressional representative. She became so active that the representative disparagingly identified her as a "ringleader." She wore that term proudly, just as many women had turned an insult to Sen. Elizabeth Warren—"nonetheless, she persisted"—into a battle cry.

In early 2018, that representative unexpectedly announced he would not be running for re-election. While Saily's immediate Goal was now moot, Saily herself was just getting started. The whole process had revealed her bigger life purpose: political activism.

Saily released her inner superhero to make that transition into a more meaningful life*. By releasing your inner superhero, you will summon the courage to take action on a step toward your Goal that may have been scary before.

x ↔⟩————————→ •

---

* Saily left her corporate job and is now the Executive Director of NJ 11th for Change. She's been featured in the New York Times, on National Public Radio and in Marie Claire. Her new Goal is to "flip the district" in the next election.

You are a superhero to someone, today and every day. You have already had a positive meaningful impact on the people around you. **You are a hero.**

If there is something you need to do as you approach your Goal, take the superhero pose. Remind yourself that you have within you what it takes to achieve your Goal. And go do it, superstar!

REFLECTION STOP POINT

× When have you taken bold, decisive action?

× When did you act with so much courage you surprised even yourself? What led to this?

ACTION STOP POINT

× Let's try this. Set a timer for two minutes, then stand up, feet shoulder-width apart, hands on your hips, chest out. Breathe deeply, and concentrate on your power. Stay focused on your strength. After the two minutes are up, write down how you feel. Did anything shift for you? What feels different for you now than it did two minutes ago?

IDENTIFY YOUR STAKEHOLDERS

Your stakeholders are the people you know and love who are directly affected by you pursuing and achieving your Goal. I briefly introduced this concept in Chapter 1 when I shared the story about Sophia, who was able to stop smoking by thinking about the impact it would have on her daughter, and again in Chapter 2 when you thought about the people who would be impacted by your achievement when you were clarifying your **SMART** Goal.

Your stakeholders are the people who will be most impacted by the change that comes with you achieving your Goal. Ideally, they are the people closest to you, who stand to gain or lose the most based on your achievement. They are the people whose well-being matters to you, the people for whom you are motivated to be your best self.

One of the most powerful stakeholder stories I've have ever heard was told to me by Jeremy, a colleague who had survived a coma after a near-death car crash. Jeremy said that while he was in the hospital, truly struggling for his life, he kept returning to thoughts of his young daughter. He kept telling himself to stay alive, to try to communicate, to do whatever he could to stay alive so that he could be there for his daughter, to be her dad again.

After coming out of his coma, and spending years of his life in physical therapy, Jeremy made a full recovery. He credits his daughter with giving him the motivation to pull away from death and toward life.

REFLECTION STOP POINT

x Have you ever heard a story like this, when someone's love for another person helped them do something they didn't think was otherwise possible? Recall the story and relive it.

x Have you ever done something incredibly difficult, motivated by your desire to see or be with a loved one?

Todd came to my office at a very interesting point in his life. He was at the cusp of retirement, planning to work another two or three years to meet his financial goals, when his company unexpectedly terminated his employment.

He wanted to use coaching to decide if he could find more work for the next few years, or pursue an early retirement. He was eager to retire (and planned to do so back in Portland, Oregon, where he had lived for more than a decade) but felt he needed a few more years of earnings on the East Coast. He had a son who was entering his senior year of high school, and who lived part time with Todd and part time with Todd's ex-wife. Todd wanted to pay for his son's education and wasn't sure he could do that without more employment.

He was also the primary caretaker for his mother, who was in her 90s; she had recently moved into a senior living center close to his home in New Jersey. Whatever decision he made, it would have a serious impact on his mother and son.

If he retired to Portland, his mother would need to be moved to the west coast, which would likely be her last cross-country trip. His son would have to finish his senior year of high school without his dad nearby.

In the end, he was able to make the best decision for himself by creating opportunities for his mother and younger son. He took his son on a college tour of Oregon schools, which piqued his son's interest.

Together they realized that they could save more in tuition if Todd moved to Oregon and his son took a gap year in Oregon to establish residency before attending University of Oregon. A gap year would give them the opportunity to travel and connect.

As for Todd's mother, he researched the senior living centers in Portland and found they were better, and more cost effective, than those in New Jersey. And if Todd retired, he could spend more time with her.
He decided that he would be happy to get by with a little less money in exchange for more time to spend riding motorcycles on the Oregon coastline, more time to spend with his mother, and creating better opportunities for his son in Oregon.

Although Todd was eager to retire, he couldn't create the momentum to do so when he took only his needs into consideration. He made his choice with confidence once he saw how it would benefit his family*.

• →————————→ *

---

* When I reached out to Todd for his approval to use this story in this book, he shared the following update: "For the past month we've [Todd and his son] been traveling around China. Last week we hiked the Tiger River Gorge in northern Yunnan province, not far from Tibet, and tomorrow we check out the terracotta warriors here in Xian. I return to Portland in a couple weeks to look after Mom while my son will stay in China and travel or work and polish up his Mandarin. Then he'll return to Oregon to start his freshman year at UO. Since I'm a regular at the Ducks football and b-ball games, I'll get to have a beer with him down there every other week or so." Todd also mentioned that he's been hired for a fair number of consulting gigs since he "retired," which he enjoys.

REFLECTION STOP POINT

× Everyone has stakeholders. Whose lives will be most affected by you achieving your Goal? If you're the breadwinner in the family, this can have a major impact. If you're an earner, even if it's not as the sole (or primary) breadwinner, how will this change impact your spouse, children, dogs, vacations, and friends—positively or negatively?

× If you're re-launching after divorce, how will this impact your children? Your future spouse? Your shared friends? If you're launching your life after college (and still living at home for now), how will this impact your parents?

ACTION STOP POINT

× Who are the people who will be impacted by you achieving or not achieving your Goal? Name at least three, along with how they will be impacted if you achieve or don't achieve your Goal.

× Do you have someone you'd like to dedicate your Goal to? Who can you honor with this achievement? Or more importantly, when the chips are down and you need a little push, whose face will give you that extra energy to keep going? By dedicating your Goal, you'll gain the momentum you need to cross the finish line.

× Now that you've identified the impact of your Goal on your stakeholders, let that knowledge motivate you to move forward with your Goal. Let the image of that person at the finish line help you pursue your Action steps today.

LET YOUR ROLE MODELS PULL YOU UP

I often encourage my clients to focus on a role model, someone they admire who helps grow their own sense of potential. After all, we are the same species that put a man on the moon; we are capable of great things individually and collectively. So, one way to keep that self-talk positive is to focus on role models, people who inspire and elevate you.

A role model can be a person who motivates you by the way they live their own lives. They inspire you to be a better version of yourself based on what they've accomplished. They've often demonstrated bravery, strength, and courage. They tend to have personal integrity and kindness. They can be someone you've heard about, or someone you know personally. Role models may have had great accomplishments, or may have risen in the face of adversity.

Most accomplished people have worked very hard to get where they are; they usually have a story of hard work underneath what seems like natural ability. Did you know Michael Jordan was cut from his high school basketball team?

Nobody is great without hard work and years of dedicated effort: just look at the real-life examples cited by author Geoff Colvin in a 2006 *Forbes* magazine story called "What it Takes to be Great."

Michael Jordan was just one case; he put himself through intense training on his own, in addition to the team practices. All-time great receiver Jerry Rice was passed up by fifteen football teams because they thought he was too slow. Rice practiced so hard that other players would get sick trying to keep up. Bobby Fischer, who became a chess master at sixteen, had been studying chess intensively for nine years. Tiger Woods started playing golf when he was just eighteen months old, so even when he won the U.S. Amateur

Championship at eighteen, he had put in over fifteen years of practice.

"The critical reality is that we are not hostage to some naturally given level of talent. We can make ourselves what we will," Colvin wrote in the Forbes article, which later became a book called *Talent is Overrated: What Really Separates World-Class Performers from Everybody Else.*

Louis Zamperini began life as an unlikely role model— he was a high-spirited kid who always seemed to be running away from trouble. His unusual speed took him to the Olympics, and then he became a fighter pilot in World War II. When his plane crashed in the Pacific Ocean, he managed to stay alive for a harrowing forty-seven days on a life raft with two other men, one of whom died before the others were captured by the Japanese. Zamperini spent the next two years as a prisoner of war, targeted by a sadistic prison guard for beatings and torture. When the war ended, Zamperini was liberated. He returned to the United States, married, and raised a family. His powerful story of strength and resilience became the subject of the book and movie *Unbroken.*

We all now know Jane Goodall as a groundbreaking anthropologist, and she had no formal scientific background when she first set out to study chimpanzees. Did you know her early work was met with resistance from British authorities? And, what's more, the chimps themselves initially fled from her when she started to observe them. Her research eventually became revolutionary, and it was the result of years of tremendous patience and persistence.

One of my role models, Martha Stewart, wasn't always the cooking, gardening, and publishing magnate that she is known as now. She became a domestic icon only after careers as a model, a stockbroker and a caterer.

When I decided I wanted to go to culinary school, with the dream of helping people gain confidence in their own kitchens, I wanted to learn from the person who did it best. I made working for Martha my single-minded focus, and I assembled all the connections I could to score an interview. Within six months, I was hired as an intern working for the then-brand-new magazine called *Every Day Food.* One month later, I was standing in the kitchen with Martha herself, tasting and evaluating dishes for the magazine. Six months after that, I was offered a full-time position as a TV Segment Chef.

And when I told Martha I wanted to write cookbooks, she didn't give me the dismissive answer that so many had before her. She replied: "I didn't even publish my first book until I was forty-one."

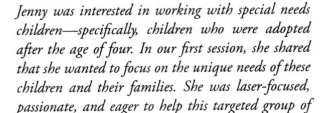

Jenny was interested in working with special needs children—specifically, children who were adopted after the age of four. In our first session, she shared that she wanted to focus on the unique needs of these children and their families. She was laser-focused, passionate, and eager to help this targeted group of people.

After Jenny shared her vision, and I acknowledged her passion and focus, she confessed that she had no idea where to start, because no one was doing the type of work she wanted to do. "Maybe so, maybe not," I said, "but who is doing work close to the kind of work you want to do?" We brainstormed different adoption agencies, child therapists, child therapists working with special needs children, and adoptive child therapists. Soon we had a long list of people who were doing work similar to what she wanted to do.

This was her list of role models, people who were a bit further down her desired path. She was eager to reach out to them, connect with them, see how they got to where they were.

Jenny was going to use these role models to develop her own unique path.

● ⤳————————→ ✴

The most powerful role model connections are often people you already know, people in your family or close circle who you can look up to. Martha Stewart was an inspiration to me, and so was my grandmother, who earned a living and was financially independent for the second half of her life. Without a college degree, without a strong work history, she used her great attitude to take responsibility for herself.

Who is a role model within your midst? Who do you know who has done something powerful? Is it your great-grandfather, who was the first in your family to put himself through college? Or is it your mother, who became a single parent and raised your family on her own? Who do you know who is brave on a regular basis, overcoming disease, raising a special needs child, or suffering from a debilitating injury? Who do you know that makes you think, "This person is incredible, *how do they do it?*"

ACTION STOP POINT

× Create a list of ten role models. They can be people you know personally, or people you have never met. Next to each person, describe why they have made your list—what quality do they have that makes them a role model?

× Now create a list of at least five people who are role models to you and are specifically connected to your Goal (like Martha Stewart was for me). This may be a subset of your existing list; the point is that they are connected to your goal.

× What have they done that makes them a role model for your list? Do you know them personally? If not, is there a way for you to meet them? Please find a way to connect with your role model, whether via Facebook, Twitter, Instagram, LinkedIn, or just reaching out and saying hello.

If you're looking for an extra burst of inspiration, a way to tune in to the incredible human being who might just live next door, let me share a little secret with you. It's called *StoryCorps*.

StoryCorps is a collection of stories, told by regular people to someone close to them. Their mission is to "preserve and share humanity's stories in order to build connections between people and create a more just and compassionate world."

Talk about a meaningful Goal! *StoryCorps* began with an actual physical "StoryBooth" in Grand Central Terminal in New York City in 2003. People were asked to bring a friend into the audio recording booth and interview that person, ask questions they'd always wanted to ask, or share a meaningful story.

To listen to *StoryCorps* stories, all you need to do is go to their web site, http://www.storycorps.org, or download their app. They are often featured on local NPR programs if you have one in their area. Today, they've published five books, including *Callings: The Purpose and Passion of Work* and *All There Is: Love Stories from StoryCorps*. They also have a powerful series of animated shorts, which they've used to bring their stories to life.

When I need inspiration, I head to *StoryCorps* and listen. There are two particularly powerful *StoryCorps* stories that have stayed with me.

One is an interview conducted by Joshua Littman, a twelve-year-old boy with Asperger's, who chose to interview his mother. He asked questions like, "Do you love me less than my sister?" "What is it like to be my mom?" "Do you wish you didn't have me?" It's a powerful interview, and it showcases a child's curiosity and a mother's strength.

The second *StoryCorps* story that resonated with me is a conversation between Mary Johnson and Oshea Israel, the man who killed her teenage son. They describe how they started their relationship and how that relationship blossomed into a kind of mother-son relationship.

As a result of this experience, Johnson founded "From Death to Life," an organization that supports mothers who've lost children to homicide, and encourages forgiveness between families of murderers and victims.

The people on *StoryCorps* are not Michael Jordan or Louis Zamperini. They are much more likely to be sitting next to you in traffic or in the stands at a soccer game. It's invigorating to think of "ordinary" people with exceptional character in our midst. There are a lot of them, too— the *StoryCorps* website has more than 400,000 stories. Have a listen.

REFLECTION STOP POINT

× If you had to invite someone you know to record a StoryCorps story with you, who would you ask? Who is the first person that comes to mind? The second? The third? Put together a list of five people.

ACTION STOP POINT

× Here's a special challenge: Choose one person from your lists above. Go to https://storycorps.org/participate/ and find out where you can record a story near you, or as a DIY.

MILESTONES & INCH PEBBLES

Some Goals are scary. And some Action steps just don't seem to get accomplished, no matter how many times they show up on your Action list. When an Action item isn't getting done, it's not time to be tough and push through it, it's time to honestly ask yourself why.

This is also a good time to use the milestones and inch pebbles tool. A milestone is a big accomplishment, like running a marathon or getting into a college of your choice. An inch pebble is a smaller accomplishment on the way to a milestone—like spending ten minutes each day for a week meditating. Pebbles and stones, inches and miles.

Unfortunately, sometimes the Action you set for yourself seems too big and intimidating, and so it just doesn't get done. Instead of creating a reasonably sized pebble, you've created a milestone. And now this big stone is blocking your path.

How can you break it down into smaller components— inch pebbles that you can achieve? Is this Action important to you? Before you do it, what do you need to do first? What do you need to prepare yourself before you can tackle this?

Write yourself a recipe. What's first, next, and so on. You'll break that milestone into inch pebbles in no time.

Inaction is often an indication that it's time to break a milestone down into inch pebbles. You will get to that milestone eventually—after all, that's the whole point of this book! To get yourself out of the inaction or stagnation, you'll have to give yourself a few easy wins—a few inch pebbles that you can claim as your achievements. Once you've gathered a few pebbles and gained some confidence, you can attack some rocks, and then the stones will start flowing. You'll find yourself engaged in a productivity avalanche in no time.

Let's say you want to find a partner and get married. You've got to start with going on a date. And then another. After a while, you'll find out what you do and don't like in a person, and you'll hone in on what you're looking for. Even if the girl who lived next door when you were twelve seemed just perfect for you, you probably won't figure that out until you do a little bit more dating off the reservation.

If you want to lose forty pounds, you have to start by losing five, six, then seven. When people try to do something very ambitious right off the bat and skip steps, moving from A to D instead of A to B, they often get frustrated and throw up their hands (think of all the people who cheat on a too-strict diet).

Like the slow-and-steady tortoise that wins the race against that cocky hare, know that by knocking off the inch pebbles you will soon reach your milestone.

REFLECTION STOP POINT

× Is there an Action item or a milestone you've set up that just isn't getting done?

ACTION STOP POINT

× If you've answered the above in the affirmative, identify several "first next steps" for breaking down that Action item into smaller inch pebbles.

QUESTIONBURST™

Because I am a coaching geek, I am a member of the International Coaching Federation, and I attend their bi-annual global event. Can you imagine the positivity in a room full of sixteen-hundred coaches from sixty-two countries? Let's just say decaf is all that's needed at that conference.

At the August 2017 conference, the keynote speaker was Hal Gregersen, the executive director of the **MIT** Leadership Center, who has spent a career studying the minds of innovators, from Steve Jobs to Jeff Bezos. His central belief is that the magic is in the questions that are asked, and his research is focused on helping people become better questioners.

QuestionBurst™ is a technique Gregersen shared with the coaches at the conference. It is a tool he designed to help corporations move through "wicked hard problems" (**MIT** is in Boston, after all) and connect with the questions that can provide promising pathways toward solutions.

You can find his complete technique (also referred to as QBurst) on his website, http://4-24project.org. This site encourages leaders to set aside four minutes every twenty-four hours, or one day a year, to ask better questions.

Here's one QBurst example from the web site: "Suppose you're having trouble gaining customer awareness for a new product. Spend four minutes asking just questions around this challenge (for example, 'Why aren't customers noticing this product? If money was no object, what could we do to change this?')."

ACTION STOP POINT

Ready to try my modified version of QuestionBurst? Let's do this!

1. Identify an opportunity, challenge, or "wicked hard problem" you'd like to work on.

2. Identify how you feel about it: positive, negative, or neutral.

3. Articulate the problem to a partner, or just verbalize it into a camera or audio recorder. Spend no more than thirty seconds on this.

4. Brainstorm questions for two full minutes. This is the heart of the exercise, and these are the rules: You may only brainstorm questions. Do not attempt to answer the questions or explain the questions. Just ask the questions. By the end of the exercise, you will likely have twelve to fifteen questions.

5. Identify how you feel about the topic now: positive, negative, or neutral? If you don't feel a bit more positive, repeat step four.

6. Sort the questions and commit to answering the ones that will move you forward: Take a look at the questions. Is there a theme or themes? Are there a few questions that are resonating with you enough that you'd like to pursue answers? Commit to a timeframe to pursue these answers.

REFLECTION STOP POINT

× How did the QuestionBurst work for you? What did you like about it? When can you see yourself using this again?

Some questions will be answerable right away or in a short period of time; others you can answer if you take them away and think about them. Others still might seem insurmountable. That's okay. Once you've worked through the easier ones, chances are you'll have some insight into the harder ones, too.

Although this technique was designed for corporate executives, I use it with my career and life coaching clients when the client feels stuck or overwhelmed, when there appears to be "too much" on their mind and they want to break free from that feeling.

Does that sound familiar? I hope so. A QuestionBurst is just a different way to explode a stuck point (like a milestone) and shatter it into smaller questions (like inch pebbles).

As an example, a client may bring a big question like this to the session: "Do I want to marry my girlfriend?" Let's start with rapid fire sub-questions like:

› What will our relationship be like in twenty years?
› How will I be able to handle her debt?
› Will she be loyal to me?
› Is she going to end up like her mom?
› Is she dependable?
› What kind of a mom is she going to be?
› Will I still be attracted to her?
› What about the fact that she loves being social and I'm more of a homebody?
› What would happen if we divorced?
› She thinks I'm messy. Is she always going to nag me about that?
› Will she contribute financially, or will I have to be the breadwinner?

If you run out of questions and there's more time left, dig deeper. That tends to be when the best stuff comes out.

In my practice, I'll write the questions on a whiteboard as my client talks. Clients always experience great relief getting those questions out of their head—often, they didn't even realize they had those questions on their minds. It's liberating! And then, once the questions are out there, they can pursue the ones they want answered. It's best to do this exercise with a partner or a recorder, so you can be free to just think without the burden of having to write everything down.

EUSTRESS

Have you read this word before? Do you know what it means? It's a marvelous tactical tool I love to use, and I have yet to find a client who has heard of this word, or concept, before I shared it. As we become a more mindful culture and world, my hope is that more people learn about eustress earlier in their lives.

Okay, I know, get to it already. So the word eustress has two components, "eu" and "stress." My assumption is that you are already keenly aware of the word stress. It can come in the form of anxiety, nervousness, or a feeling that the walls are closing in or that you're treading water.

Uplifting, eh? Stay with me. "Eu" is a Greek root that means "good" or "well." You see the same root in the words "euphoria," "euphemism," and "euphony." So if you put the two parts of the word together, you get a positive type of stress.

Positive stress? You bet. Like that feeling of nervousness before an interview or before you ask someone out on a date. Before the prom, or your first day of school, or traveling to a new country.

Eustress is good for you! It's the heightened sense of awareness that primes you to be alert, preparing you to perform at your best.

So when you experience that feeling of stress before doing something big, the question is: How do you meet and greet it? Think about a football coach talking to the team at halftime. The players may be down, and he uses his platform to shift their energy into positive action. He takes the stress they may be feeling about losing and turns it into eustress, where the entire group is aligned toward a common goal.

If you are preparing for a speech and feel stress, how can you shift that into eustress—something that feeds your power for the speech?

Feeling anxiety related to a specific event, like a job interview or sending an email to someone who can help you, is a good tip that it's important to you. It's important, so it's causing you stress. Instead of letting anxiety get the better of you, find a way to flip it to be eustress—you at your best, primed to deliver, using that extra awareness to enhance your talent.

REFLECTION STOP POINT

× Can you identify a moment during this process when you felt nervousness or anxiety and used that extra energy to propel yourself forward? How did that work to your benefit?

MEDITATION

When did meditation go mainstream? It's such a powerful cultural meme that it's now part of preschool and elementary curriculums. I often recommend mindfulness meditation to my clients when it seems like their thoughts and emotions are taking over their minds

I use the following example to demonstrate when it's time for a meditation intervention. Think about a dog owner walking their dog on a leash. Sometimes the dog is in charge, and the owner is just trailing after the dog, like the tail of a kite. Ideally, the owner is in charge, and the dog feels calmer and safer as a result.

Does your brain control what you think, what you put the energy of your mind toward? Or do you choose your thoughts actively?

Headspace is a meditation app I often recommend to my clients. It's easy to start—Headspace only asks you to commit to meditating for ten minutes a day. It also has short, useful videos to explain mindfulness. With this kind of meditation, you allow unpleasant thoughts to come and go without getting too invested in or distracted by each one. The listener is advised to acknowledge unpleasant thoughts without letting them take over.

When left to their own devices, our minds can pursue any number of distractions, and this is only enhanced by social media and pervasive screens. Meditation helps us to respond instead of react. For example, if you are driving and someone cuts you off, you're going to be distracted by what just happened. There's a sense of fear, aggravation, possibly anger. Do you choose to say, "What an asshole! What is wrong with him?!" How long do you let his behavior impact your mood? With mindfulness, you learn to observe the aggravation, without following it.

You take responsibility for your own emotional and psychological landscape. Mindfulness pulls you out of reactivity (where you get immediately captivated and distracted by the things that happen) and into responsiveness (where you have an opportunity to decide what you'll think about).

Many negative reactions, such as losing our temper or hitting something, may feel involuntary. With meditation practice, you can learn over time to exercise more control over your actions, to have responsiveness instead of reactivity.

Headspace is my choice because it's easy and effective. The owner of the company and host of the meditation, Andy Puddicombe, is a pleasant-sounding guy. There are other similar apps; Simple Habit does five-minute meditations, and Aura does three-minute ones. So if you are an anxious person and you struggle to set aside your worries and meditate for any length of time, three minutes might be the way to go. There are also similar guided meditation videos on Amazon Prime, and there's a YouTube channel called "Honest Guy's Meditation" that people love. Once you decide to do mindfulness meditation, there are a ton of different options, so play around and find what works for you.

Meditation is something you do for you, as opposed to the things you do for other people. Of course, as I mentioned earlier, a better you is better for your stakeholders, so in the end, they'll gain from this too. Mindfulness meditation, in particular, helps clear your mind. Our minds get cluttered, just like a desk, so it can be good to take a couple minutes every day to clear everything off, and then decide what gets to go back on.

x →————————→ •

Daniel was waking up multiple times every night. Each time he woke up, he would be racked with anxiety about all the things he needed to do. I suggested that he write down his thoughts in effort to capture them, so he could let them go. When the thoughts woke him up he would say, "Hello, thoughts. You are important! But I'm going to be better addressing you after a good night's sleep. I will see you when I wake up at eight o'clock." These thoughts don't get to keep you up at night. Be the boss of your brain.

That was somewhat effective, and he wanted more. He tried making the list before he went to bed, and then doing a Headspace meditation before he drifted to sleep. That did the trick.

● ↪——————————→ ✿

If you're having a chocolate craving, you don't have to just automatically throw chocolate in your mouth like a chocolate-eating zombie. You can ask, "Why do I have this craving? Is it the caffeine, the antioxidants, the sugar?" Then you can decide what you actually need.

INSIGHTS & ACTION

INSIGHTS

> What was most useful for you in this chapter to motivate you toward your Goal? What comes to mind without looking back?

Turn back the pages, review the headings. Look at the topics that you circled or highlighted. What was most useful?

1.

2.

3.

4.

5.

ACTIONS

> › Which tool or tools will grease the wheels as you drive toward your Goal?
> › Choose at least one of the tactical tools from this chapter and work it.

Identify at least three Actions steps that you would like to take toward your Goal.

1.
2.
3.

PREP SHEET

Please complete the following questions before you begin the next chapter:

MY GOAL IS:

....

....

WHERE AM I, ON A SCALE OF 1 TO 10, TOWARD ACHIEVING MY GOAL?

| 1 | 2 | 3 | 4 | 5 | 6 | 7 | 8 | 9 | 10 |

WHAT HAVE I ACCOMPLISHED SINCE I BEGAN READING CHAPTER 7?

....

....

WHAT DIDN'T I GET DONE, BUT INTENDED TO DO?

....

....

WHAT OPPORTUNITIES ARE AVAILABLE TO ME RIGHT NOW?

....

....

BY THE END OF THE NEXT CHAPTER I WANT TO:

....

....

ANY INSIGHTS OR NEW AWARENESS THAT EXCITES ME?

....

....

EIGHT

CLOSE THE DEAL

CLOSE THE DEAL

×⟶⟶⟶⟶⟶ ●

Congratulations! You've arrived at a "9" on your "How close am I to achieving this Goal" scale. You are close enough to see it. If you're not yet at this point, circle back to Chapters 6 and 7, or even the Happiness or Networking chapters. Choose what you think will help you get closer to your goal. And if it's time to pick up the phone and call on the help of a mentor, or even the services of a real live coach, do it.

In this chapter, you will acknowledge what you've done to get here, create a strategy to take this one over the finish line with a smile on your face, connect with why this Goal matters to you, and authentically deliver your final Actions.

I'm *kvelling** over here. I'm so proud of you for getting to this place. As it is said, it's the voyage, not arriving at the

---

* *Kvelling* is Yiddish word that describes the feeling of being extraordinarily pleased, bursting with joy, a great sense of pride.

destination, that matters. The hardest of the hard work is behind you. You are ready and prepared for your next step.

First, let's take a moment to acknowledge what you've done and how you've come to this point.

REFLECTION STOP POINT

× How much time have you spent actively working toward this Goal? When did you start?

× Take a look at what you've done. What are a couple Actions you've taken that you're proud of?

× Which Action that you took surprised you the most?

× How is your life different now than it was when you began pursuing this Goal?

WHAT A "9" FEELS LIKE

Now that you've arrived at this point, you must be *kvelling* too. You're at a "9"! It's the feeling you have when you're in your third round of interviews at the company you want to work for. It's the feeling of a musician who has thoroughly practiced her piece and is sitting in front of a live audience, ready to perform.

If you watch the Olympics, you can see that "9" impatience and readiness in top athletes. I can still remember Mary Lou Retton running toward the vault in the 1984 Summer Olympics. She needed a score of 10 to win the all-around gold medal, and you could tell in the intensity of her run that she had it. Despite a recent knee injury, she approached the vault at just the right speed, with a strong stride and total focus. As I watched, I knew she had it. Everyone knew she had it. When you're approaching your 10, remember Mary Lou, running toward that vault.

REVERSE ENGINEER YOUR GOAL

So, what's left? What are the final pieces you need to put in place before you achieve your Goal? To reverse engineer it, instead of thinking toward your Goal, back up from your Goal.

Start by imagining yourself having achieved the Goal. Think about that moment when you've done it. Maybe it's finding out you're pregnant, or receiving the call that they'd like to offer you that job (with the signing bonus you asked for), or receiving a letter of acceptance from the grad school program you want to attend.

Now, take a step back in time. What was the last step you took before achieving your Goal? What was the step before that, and the step before that?

If you do this slowly enough, reverse engineering your Goal, you'll create a backwards recipe you can follow to get to your Goal.

ACTION STOP POINT

× What actions are left for you to take toward your Goal? Walk yourself backwards, starting from achieving your Goal, and identify the remaining steps that are needed. Voice record or video record your plan.

CREATE YOUR STRATEGY (OR STRATEGIES)

Dwight D. Eisenhower is credited with saying, "Plans are worthless, but the process of planning is everything." Although you don't know for sure what the future will bring, you can think through what you'd like to have. You can create Plans A, B, and C, backup plans, and backups for your backups. By preparing yourself for what might happen and creating options, you're putting yourself in a mindset to ensure this happens.

Now that you've reverse engineered your goal, let's create a few more options.

Let's borrow some thinking from the world of football. You're the quarterback, and your team is on the ten-yard line, with the ability to score if you do the right things. There are a few possible ways to get there. What's one way? What's another way that could also work? The coach has been drilling these plays into you.

REFLECTION STOP POINT

× Do you have more than one plan to pursue your Goal at this point? Identify several options before you move forward.

WHAT'S THE BIG PICTURE GOAL?

If your Goal is to be happier at work, hopefully you've been job hunting *and* looking for ways to improve your current job. If you're trying to determine whether you want to stay in your marriage or not, hopefully you've been meeting with divorce lawyers *and* seeing a marriage counselor. By creating multiple avenues to achieve your Goal, you can make the best possible choice.

With clients who are looking to make a job change, I rarely have them focus on just one job. They pursue multiple jobs (and don't stop the pursuit until the job offer is accepted), because the only thing better than a terrific job offer is multiple, concurrent, terrific job offers. And, of course, negotiating with multiple offers on the table puts them in a position of strength.

This strategy goes far beyond job seeking. First, it recognizes that people are complex, and often no single endeavor will fulfill their needs. And second, it often creates clarity. By fully following that nagging feeling that you "should" have been a gym teacher, you may be able to better determine whether you want to pivot your career—or whether that urge would be better satisfied by becoming a volunteer Little League coach.

x ◆⟩————————⟩ ●

Paisley, a UI (user interface) designer, was talented, and she knew it. She had a solid, well-paying job working for a big company, and a three-hour commute. She had two young children, and she wanted to shorten her commute while still doing similar work.

In our work together, she identified companies that would require a shorter commute. She networked, and landed an interview. While she didn't make a spectacular impression, it was enough to receive a job offer. The corporation offered her a good, solid opportunity with a terrific team—at a lower salary.

She wanted everything about this offer except a pay cut. This was tough for her because it was a much shorter commute, a better team, and a stronger corporate culture. This job was an 80 percent improvement.

She was at a "9". She had a job offer. She also had to lean into that feeling that something was missing. She realized she owed it to herself to negotiate for more money, and if the company said no, she could then decide if she still wanted the job. She had nothing to lose.

Paisley put together a strong case for why she deserved a higher salary and gave it her best shot. It worked. The company agreed to give her the pay she asked for. That made her choice easy.

And here's the best part: not even a year later, a consulting company poached Paisley from the new company because of her outstanding work with her old company. They offered her a position to bring her back as a consultant at her old company, with a pay increase and a more flexible schedule.

Paisley didn't achieve her Goal, she exceeded it.

● ⋅→⟶ → ✳

CLOSING THE DEAL: BE AUTHENTIC

As you approach your Goal, it can be tempting to do "whatever it takes" to close the deal. I believe it's a lot sweeter to achieve your Goal with authenticity. You set the goal from a place of truth, now let that truth, and your values take you the final mile.

x ⋅→⟶ → ●

Remember Scott, the client I mentioned in Chapter 2 who thought I tricked him into recognizing that his life was pretty good after he completed the Whole

Life Model? He's a terrific example of the benefits of being yourself.

Scott had a friend who told him about a job with one of the leading global banks, and he knew it was exactly what he wanted. He was able to get an interview, and asked me to dedicate a coaching session to prepare for it. When he walked into my office he said, "I got this. My friend told me I should say this and that, basically tell them what they want to hear."

So I asked him why he came in for a coaching session if he knew what he wanted to say. We both knew he wanted to get that job and that he had the skills for it. And he knew that I wouldn't let him lie.

I said, "Tell me why you want this job so badly." Once we got past the obvious (he was out of work and needed money to take care of his newborn son), he dug deeper. At first, Scott said, "It's a good job, it's where I belong." He was having a hard time getting it out, and finally he made the connection; the finance company he had worked at for seven years was a bond bucket shop, the kind of first-tier broker dealers that are somewhat shady and now disappearing. It wasn't a place where he saw growth opportunities; the company wasn't going in a good direction.

Scott was now interviewing at a prestigious global bank. Bond trading was just one small part of the bank's operations. He could grow, learn, and excel based on his hard work and outstanding attitude. It was a solid company with a good reputation. And he was perfect for it—he had a great memory, he had strong relationship skills, and he loved the industry. Plus, this company was an easy commute from his house.

He was soon able to articulate why he was a perfect fit for the job, based on the experiences he had, the person he was, and the employee he could become.

By the time he left my office, he couldn't wait for that interview. He could articulate why he was uniquely qualified for the job and how he hoped to be a long-term contributor to the organization.

This was a complete turnaround from where we started the session, with him wanting to just say anything to get the job. He had been mistreated at his prior shop and was behaving inauthentically because that was the culture of his last company.

In our session, he gained comfort that he could show his true colors in the interview and get the job. He was at his "9", ready for that interview, and he figured out exactly what he needed to do to land the job and start it on the right foot.

He was given a verbal offer at the end of the interview. When he received his written offer, the salary exceeded his target by twenty thousand dollars, plus a generous overtime and bonus package.

× What will achieving this Goal do for you? How does it reflect your values? How can you use your values to pursue these final Action steps?

WHISTLE WHILE YOU WORK

Some Goals take time to accomplish. If you're trying to lose a hundred pounds in a healthy way, that will likely take more than a year. As you see yourself moving steadily in the right direction, what can you do to celebrate your ongoing achievements?

Do you want to invest in some new pieces for your wardrobe? Try a new hairstyle? Reconnect with old friends? Travel to a place you've never been?

Hopefully, the successes you've achieved to this point have bolstered your confidence, as you accomplished inch pebble achievements on the way to your milestone. You're not far from the finish line now, so you see yourself walking right up to it knowing you've earned it.

While there will be a lot of celebrating when you cross the finish line in the next chapter, it's also important to recognize the work that you put in every step of the way. You're working hard, and you need to find a way to give back to yourself.

Part of that last push will involve self-care and positive reinforcement, whether that comes from you acknowledging what you've done, or others in your life recognizing it. Sometimes your friends and family will know what you need, other times you'll need to ask them for what you need. Either way, make sure you're getting the care you need for this final stretch.

REFLECTION STOP POINT

- × How can you refill your tanks before you take this final step?

- × Who would you like to take a moment with, to share what you've achieved?

- × Who has been noticing the change in you?

FINAL THOUGHTS

As I mentioned in the opening lines of this chapter, right now you are standing in the wings, waiting to take the stage. Whenever you're about to go on stage, there is always someone there to give you your cue and some encouragement, whether it's a hearty smile, "have fun," "go get 'em," or "break a leg." That's the last thing that happens before you're ushered into your spotlight.

You are here. You're waiting in the wings. You're Mary Lou approaching the vault. It's like you're about to have a baby; the doctor and nurses can actually see him, and they're telling you to give it **One. Last. Push.**

INSIGHTS & ACTIONS

INSIGHTS

- › As you read the chapter, which ideas and stories resonated most deeply with you?
- › How do you plan to celebrate when you achieve your Goal?

› Who or what is inspiring you, right now, to make your Goal a reality?

1.

2.

3.

4.

5.

ACTIONS

Identify the remaining steps to your Goal and make them happen.

1.

2.

3.

4.

5.

PREP SHEET

At this point, you have achieved your Goal.

Take a few moments to appreciate what you've done, raise your hands over your head, and jump up and down a few times. Have your end zone celebration. Shout it out loud and proud. **You did it.**

ENJOY THE FEELING OF RATING YOUR PROGRESS TOWARDS ACHEIVING YOUR GOAL AT A 10!

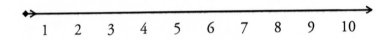

That's all the prep you need before you begin the final chapter.

NINE

CELEBRATE, REST, AND REPEAT

CELEBRATE, REST, AND REPEAT

You did it! In this chapter, you will take some time to acknowledge what you've achieved and celebrate it. I'll help you find ways to share the win with those who've helped you and those who will be thrilled to learn of your accomplishment. I'll share the positive impact that acknowledging and celebrating your Goal will have on you, those around you, and the next Goal you set. And before we conclude (I'm not ready for this to end!), I'll highlight the value of a well-deserved rest, both after this accomplishment and on a regular basis.

LOOKING BACK OVER YOUR TRIP—THE HERO'S JOURNEY

Famed mythologist Joseph Campbell wrote about the Hero's Journey, a narrative structure of many myths. In his book, *The Hero with a Thousand Faces*, he described it like this:

"A hero ventures forth from the world of common day into a region of supernatural wonder: fabulous forces are there encountered, and a decisive victory is won: the hero comes back from this mysterious adventure with the power to bestow boons on his fellow man."

The hero, or protagonist, starts on his journey because of an interruption or a change—he receives a call to action. He also has to meet people and be outfitted with wisdom, tools, or weapons for his journey. In the supernatural realm, the hero encounters completely unexpected circumstances and has to find the resources within himself to overcome the ensuing obstacles and monsters. As the hero overcomes each obstacle, he is transformed a little bit more into that hero archetype. Finally, he encounters one final obstacle, one last monster, to reach his goal. Having done that, he is usually able to bring a boon, magical artifact, or miracle, back to his people.

Campbell wrote this narrative arc as a universal story, one that could be matched to folk tales from cultures all over the world. Campbell believed there are certain universal symbols and stories that are common to every human culture. He believed that we share an unconscious heritage, rich with symbolic language we can all access.

And now, this structure applies to your story. Like the hero in the myth, you, too, have traveled a path, overcome, and succeeded.

ACTION STOP POINT

x Write down your Goal, and then write down what you actually achieved.

x Is there a difference?

× Did you do more? Did you make a shift?

× What is the impact on you? On your stakeholders?

× How is your life different now than when you picked up this book?

× Think back on the timeline of this event; take a moment to sit with each occurrence in your journey to reach your Goal. Reviewing the Insights and Actions and the end of the chapter, and rereading each prep sheet is a terrific way to take stock of your journey.

ACKNOWLEDGE YOUR ACHIEVEMENT & CHANGE YOUR BRAIN

You have envisioned this moment from the day you began this book. While you read, you answered questions about this moment—what it would feel like, where you would be, and who you would share it with.

You are now here.

This is a moment that, unfortunately, tends to get short shrift for many people for a variety of reasons. Some keep it as a private victory, because singing your own praises can be misunderstood as haughty and arrogant. Others don't have time to celebrate; they just move on to the next thing.

There is a concept in neuroscience called neuroplasticity, which essentially means that the brain becomes what the brain does. It means your brain can change throughout your life, and the activity that usually occurs in one area can actually be transferred to another area. Your brain can even reallocate resources based on what you ask it to do.

Take Stevie Wonder, the legendary blind singer and pianist. Because he is blind, he isn't using his visual cortex. However, his perception of sound is extraordinarily developed, as is his ability to move his hands to play piano. This may be because the part of his brain usually associated with sight has actually been shifted to enable his complex piano fingering and sense of touch.

You can cause your brain to pivot from being anxious and preoccupied to being confident and productive by changing the way you act, and then realizing and recognizing the benefit of acting in a new way.

By reflecting on your accomplishment, you're reinforcing the action you took and the tools you used to make it happen. The more you sink into your successes, the more prepared you are to mobilize those tools to create future success. The more you recognize that you can do hard things, the more likely are you to do the next hard thing.

After you've achieved a Goal, you're prepared to move on to something more difficult, something that would have seemed out of reach before you achieved that first Goal. This is the mastery concept I shared in Chapter 6. When you were a child, you learned to walk. That was hard; it took months of single-minded focus and practice, and now you walk every day without giving it much thought. Now, you can run, jump, and ride a bicycle.

The first time you try something new and encounter rejection, it's hard. Think about the first time you were told "no" for a job, or rejected by the college you wanted to attend. The more rejection you encountered, hopefully, the better you became at bouncing back from it, and the more resilience you built. I mean, think about it—how many times did you fall when learning to walk? And yet, you kept trying.

You may have been nervous in Chapters 4 and 5 with those first few phone calls or outreach emails. Once you received a little positive reinforcement, you fell into the flow of it—and maybe you even enjoyed it. Those are skills you'll certainly call on in the future.

If you'd like to read more about neuroplasticity, I highly recommend *The Brain That Changes Itself: Stories of Personal Triumph from the Frontiers of Brain Science* by psychiatrist and psychoanalyst Norman Doidge.

CELEBRATE & SHARE YOUR ACHIEVEMENT

Now that you've reached your Goal, you may be a little buzzy. Friends may have already observed something different about you. People will be more attracted to you because you are thriving.

When you improve your own world, you will also improve the world for those around you. Any Goal you achieve has a ripple effect. The people around you may be motivated to make their own independent improvements. If your Goal is to start your own business, you may have relatives and friends who will see that success and be inspired to strike out on their own as well. They'll learn resilience and resourcefulness from you.

In most cultures, there are specific, recognized milestones we know how to celebrate: coming-of-age birthdays ("sweet 16s," quinceañeras, bar/bat mitzvahs), graduating high school, getting married, having a baby. We also know how to celebrate cultural holidays like Ramadan, Easter, Martin Luther King Day, Thanksgiving, Chinese New Year, and Rosh Hashana.

We have small private moments that segue into bigger celebrations, such as the moment you find out you're pregnant or when you get engaged. Then there are the quiet moments that we're less sure how to celebrate—earning an A on a test, getting a raise, making a sports team, or landing the lead role in a play. Sometimes we find it hard to celebrate things that we achieved on our own; it can feel self-centered or even self-congratulatory, especially when others close to us didn't have the same achievement. These small celebrations are inch pebbles on the way to larger achievements. It's not a bad thing to celebrate your achievements; the question is, what's the best way to do it?

Group celebrations are an important part of every culture and a way to connect with those around us. Imagine watching your favorite team at a sports bar. Let's say you're watching football, and a guy gets tackled; or you're watching soccer, and the player misses the goal. The entire bar reacts; you can hear a collective groan.

Let's be clear: these fans are not *in* the game, they're not even *at* the game. They still *feel the loss physically*, in their body. Let's look at the inverse: a baseball player hits a home run, a final goal is scored with seconds left to go in overtime. The bar will light up; the patrons are filled with a sense of shared achievement.

You have fans, too. There are people who have been rooting for you this whole time. In fact, a couple of them may have given you an assist! When you share your achievement with them, they will experience it as if your achievement is their achievement; your good news is their good news. You are the team they are rooting for. When you win the game, or achieve your Goal, they feel it too. They literally have skin in your game.

Remember the concept of *shepping nachas* from Chapter 5? This is that moment. By sharing your achievement, you allow others to share your joy.

REFLECTION STOP POINT

× Look back on Chapters 4 and 5. Who were the people who you wanted to reach out to? Did you?

× During the process, who helped you achieve your Goal?

× Who else do you want to share your success with?

× How would you like to share your success? Phone call? Email? Special gift? Throw a party?

ACTION STOP POINT

× To acknowledge your achievement, choose something that will let you absorb and remember this moment and feel that sensation of contentment throughout your body. This may be a special victory walk or a vacation, a piece of art for your home, or selecting a song as "your song" for this moment in time. This experience or item will remind you of what you've achieved and how you've achieved it, so you can feel the joy inside your body.

Here's an example of how *not* to celebrate. (I know, so negative!) Here's my only "don't make the mistakes I made, kid!" moment, so indulge me if you will.

When I completed my first solo cookbook, *You Can Trust a Skinny Cook*, I received a copy in the mail. I opened it by myself. I started critiquing. I didn't like the cover, or the layout, or the feel of the book. The font was too light and difficult to read. I was in critic mode, and I didn't let myself enjoy the moment.

When we officially launched the book, I heard from friends all over the country who were kind enough to buy it. They made a big fuss over the book, supported my effort, and told me how excited they were. They started using the recipes and telling me how the book helped them.

I only began to enjoy the achievement of writing a book after I saw the impact it had on the people who read it. *Boy, did I miss out!*

I wrote that book so it would be useful for people—as I hope this one is—and I didn't reinforce the joy of writing the book in and of itself. That said, I enjoyed writing the book and sharing stories. I ate all the recipes (and the mistakes). The book was years in the making, based on the favorite recipes of my cooking students. It was a culmination of a decade of work and I was proud of every ingredient that went into each recipe.

And yet, I forgot to remember those things when I saw the book. I just saw the font, the typos, and I put it down. *Talk about a missed opportunity!* So do as I say, not as I did—take this moment, and make it about **you** (even if it's just for five minutes!) and what you did to get to this place.

Ten years later, I can appreciate my first book in a new way. When I come home from work and my babysitter is preparing a recipe from my book with my children, I am filled with joy. I wanted to write that book to help people feel good about cooking, to feel competent, creative, and skilled. I didn't know these imaginary people at the time I was writing the book and, as it turns out, they were my very own family.

As a result of writing that book, my five-year-old can make a killer shrimp and pea risotto, and my three-year old slurps down her vongole. My aunt raves about the flourless chocolate cake, and my rabbi's wife never fails to compliment my black bean soup. I never imagined my book would have an effect like that, because I didn't yet know most of these people.

So that's a long way of saying: This meaningful, important Goal you just achieved will have an impact on people you haven't even met yet. They will be people who you love; you just don't know them yet. People will be impacted by what you did.

REFLECTION STOP POINT

- × At this point, think of someone else whose life will be significantly impacted by what you do. How will your Goal touch other people's lives?

- × Cement these achievements, claim this experience, so you can remember that feeling five, ten, twenty years down the road, when you'll enjoy it at a completely different level.

Do you remember Chapter 1, when I asked about a time when you felt good? I asked you to recall an achievement that you remember from when you were young. I wanted you to reconnect with it so you could feel that rush of satisfaction, confidence, joy. That memory was a touchstone for important emotions that encourage new behaviors.

This is your chance to make another memory like that.

When you recalled the times you did something well, you pulled together memories of your best self. You can gather strength when you see yourself as your very own role model, keying into the best moments of your life. No matter how far back you need to go, this will push you forward.

So acknowledge this moment, this achievement in your life. Recognize it now, so you call on it later.

And by acknowledging this achievement now, you might just make it a habit moving forward. It can be helpful to make a practice of reflecting every so often—whether it's for the New Year, your birthday, or the beginning or end of summer. By reviewing your accomplishments and progress, you're solidifying and reinforcing both the achievement and the Actions you took to get there. You'll help your brain remember, so you can more easily call it up next time.

GIVE IT A REST

In some weddings, after a bride and groom are officially married, they spend some time alone. In the olden days, there was a specific reason for this private time, since the couple had never been alone before. Sometimes it led to a bundle of joy nine months later.

In more modern times, it's a nice opportunity to take a break from the chaos of the wedding, to center yourselves as a couple, refocus, and remember what all the fuss is about: the two of you combining your lives, starting a new path together. In the Jewish tradition this is called *yichud*, which means seclusion.

My husband and I were married in my parents' backyard in North Carolina, on the banks of a river. For our *yichud*, we walked over to their dock, toasted our marriage, and slurped down some oysters* my friends Tamar and Kevin had brought from their farm in Cape Cod. After half an hour, we returned to the party with all our guests and celebrated. That time together helped us slow down and appreciate what we had just done. As a result, we were better able to celebrate with our guests.

Unfortunately, many feel unwilling—or unable—to stop and take a break. Pressures of work, social expectations, it's hard to get off the work wheel when it seems more efficient to move on to doing the next thing. So let's look at the concept of rest—historically and cross culturally.

In agrarian societies, there were seasonal feast days and holidays. Holidays were truly "holy" days, when you

---

* Yeah, I know. Not kosher. But oh so good...

stopped work and gathered yourself to pray, which was ideally a focusing communal activity. Feast days were when the community came together to celebrate. Rest and rejuvenation was built into the calendar, as a community. Now, I hear so many clients saying "I need a holiday from my holiday!" People come home from tropical vacations burnt out, tired, over-extended, and sick. It's helpful to treat rest like a regulatory practice, a natural part of your body's rhythm—like sleep.

REFLECTION STOP POINT

- × How often do you get rest? Daily? Weekly? Monthly? When do you do your best resting and restoring?

We've all had that winter cold that wouldn't go away, and we knew "if we could just take a couple days off work," we would get better. For whatever reason, we didn't take those days off, and that cold lasted for weeks. Athletes understand the importance of rest to achieve peak performance. Travelers plan to deal with jet lag so they can have the best travel experience.

Hundreds of years ago, we were forced into the rhythm of day and night, summer and winter. When it got dark, you went to bed. You didn't have a choice, since you couldn't see anything. In the winter, when your body had to work harder to stay warm, the nights were longer and you slept more. In the summer, when you had more energy, the nights were shorter and you could get more done while the sun was still in the sky.

Unfortunately, ever since we mastered artificial light, discovered stimulants like caffeine, and created mobile offices via computer, we've been able to work all night and all weekend.

If you've ever experienced an electrical blackout for a few days, you may have noticed that you can actually get to sleep at eight o'clock in the evening when it's dark. Without light stimulation, that's what your body naturally wants to do.

When we sleep, our brains perform neurological repair. Studies show that during sleep, the brain synthesizes and sorts through new information, so that after solid sleep we are better prepared to act on the information we received the day before. It's why people like to "sleep on it" before they make a decision. When you are able to experience the eustress of life followed by the repairing nature of rest, you are able to grow and thrive.

In many cultures, women receive postpartum care after they give birth. They are able to rest and transition from being responsible for themselves to becoming a mother. People often visit and let you share the birth story so you can revisit the process of giving birth. Hopefully it was a positive memory of strength and meaning. Even if it wasn't, it's helpful to sort through what happened. There was so much going on at the time that you might not have had time to process; now is the new mother's opportunity to sort those memories into a narrative and claim it.

By taking this moment, the mother is better prepared to move on to what's next for her in her new identity as mother. Many cultures have established a "fourth trimester," or one hundred days of rest, before a mother is expected to jump into the abundant tasks of caring for a newborn.

You'll know you've rested enough when you're itching to get back to it. If you took long, unplanned summers as a kid, you'll remember that feeling at the end of August you were a little bored and ready to get back into a routine (and so were your parents).

While you rest, pay attention to the difference between feeling in need of rest and actually feeling rested. Next time, you'll know when you need take a break before you hit that breaking point. You'll give yourself what replenishes you, whether it's spending time with friends or withdrawing for some solo downtime.

YOU'VE PROVEN YOU'RE CAPABLE OF GREATNESS

At this point, you've proven something to yourself. You know now how strong you are, what you're capable of. And you know that if you've done something once, you can do it again. By acknowledging, connecting, celebrating, and resting, you're set up for your next adventure.

ACTION STOP POINT

× Ask yourself: What change didn't you anticipate that has been impactful? What's an unexpected benefit to this Goal?

× As part of your acknowledgement, complete the Whole Life exercise again and rescore yourself. This may help you see which areas of your life have been positively impacted by this exercise and open your eyes to something you want to work on after you rest.

× Is something coming to mind that you'd like to work on as your next Goal? You don't have to start now (please don't), just acknowledge and identify that thing you might want to do next.

FROM ME TO YOU

Congratulations on finishing this book—and achieving your goal! Please, connect with me via my web site (www. allisontask.com) or on social media (www.facebook.com/ allisontask or @allisontask on Twitter), and share your achievement! You (yes, you!) are the reason I wrote this book. So let me know how this all went for you—I am ready to *shep nachas*. I'm part of your extended network, and I want to share in your success.

INSIGHTS & ACTIONS

INSIGHTS

For your final Insights exercise and to help you acknowledge your accomplishment, take your time with the following questions:

› Who gave you support and love while you were pursuing your Goal? Who helped you in other ways?
› When did you feel flow?
› Which characteristics did you exhibit to achieve your Goal? Resilience, determination, confidence, bravery, patience? All of these?
› Where did you come from, and how far have you traveled? What was your hero's journey?
› Why is this achievement important to you? What is the greater, long-lasting meaning of this accomplishment in your life?
› How did you persevere? What got you through the rough patches? What did you find most motivating?

> What's the difference in the journey when you are looking forward at it versus now, when you're looking back at it?

1.

2.

3.

4.

5.

ACTIONS

> Rescore yourself on the whole life model
> Acknowledge
> Share your news with those who've helped you (me too, please!)
> Celebrate

1.

2.

3.

4.

5.

ABOUT THE AUTHOR

I'm Allison Task, and I believe in people. As corny as it sounds, that's the simple truth. All my life, I've been a "let's do this!" kinda gal, and found that when I pursued the things I wanted to do, life was more fun. Now, I help my clients create the lives they want to live.

For the last 12 years, I've run a successful career and life coach practice, helping hundreds of clients radically transform their lives. By actively pursuing meaningful personal and career goals, my clients have changed careers, launched companies, retired early, moved around the world, and reconceived their lives, relationships, and careers.

I'm a graduate of Cornell University, and earned a coaching certificate and Master's degree from New York University. Prior to coaching, I worked in digital marketing, went to culinary school, hosted three cooking shows, and authored two cookbooks. I live with my husband and four children in Montclair, N.J.

CPSIA information can be obtained
at www.ICGtesting.com
Printed in the USA
LVOW12*2230070518
576379LV00004B/11/P